The Point of the Graver

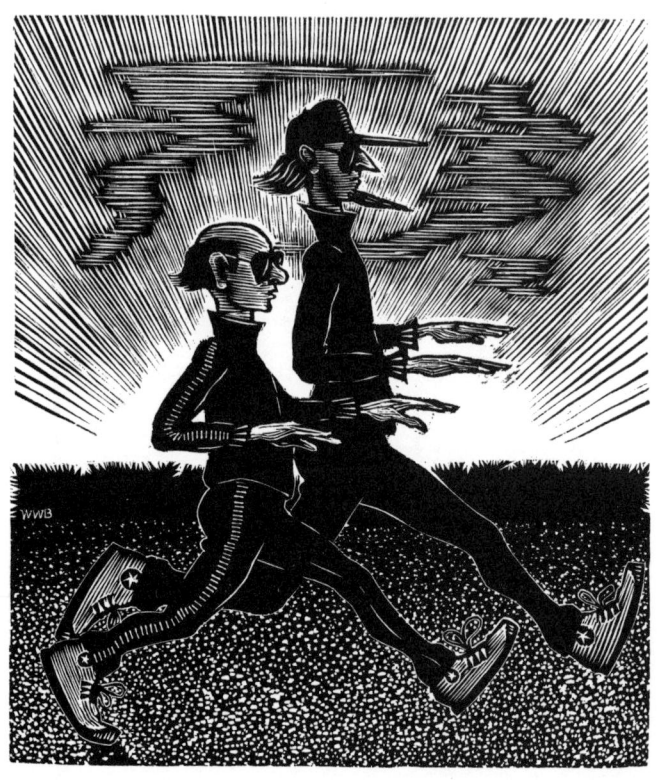

THE POINT OF THE GRAVER

Wesley W. Bates

To Don

From
Wesley Bates '94

The Porcupine's Quill, Inc.

CANADIAN CATALOGUING IN PUBLICATION DATA

Bates, Wesley W., 1952-
    The point of the graver

ISBN 0-88984-182-9

1. Bates, Wesley W.   I. Title.

NE1113.5.B3A4 1994   769.92   C94-930956-7

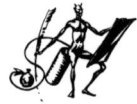

Published by The Porcupine's Quill, Inc., 68 Main St., Erin,
Ontario N0B 1T0, with financial assistance from The Canada
Council and the Ontario Arts Council. The support of the
Government of Ontario through the Ministry of Culture,
Tourism and Recreation is also gratefully acknowledged.

Represented in Canada by the Literary Press Group.
Trade orders available from General Distribution Services in
Canada (Toronto) and the United States (Niagara Falls).

Readied for the press by Paul Caulfield.
Copy edited by Doris Cowan.

To family, friends, and all
who have supported and encouraged me.

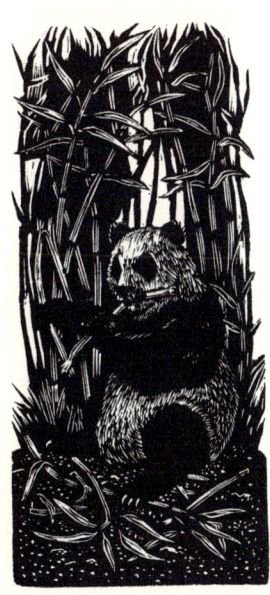

A carefully squared block of highly polished endgrain boxwood or maple and a few sharpened gravers are insignificant in themselves. But in the hands of an artist like Wesley Bates these seemingly inflexible, *demanding* materials can create form, fluidity, mood, depth: an infinite world of light and shadow, monochrome and colour.

Wesley Bates was born in Whitehorse, Yukon, in 1952. He studied fine art at Mount Allison University, New Brunswick, majoring in painting and printmaking, and he intended to pursue a career as a painter. In 1980 his wife, Katherine, gave Wesley a full set of gravers and he became fascinated with their potential. Wesley remembers that as a child he had looked at Fritz Eichenberg's engravings for *Wuthering Heights* and *Jane Eyre* and had admired their sense of the fantastic and grotesque. When he began engraving he felt the wheel had turned full circle.

The English wood engraver Clare Leighton once wrote, 'Of all media, wood-engraving is the one in which there is the least to be taught and the most to be learnt.' The engraver's challenge, to engrave light onto the block and to respect the mystery of solid blacks and whites, is not easily met; but Wesley learned his craft carefully and methodically. He looked at the work of John Farleigh, Rockwell Kent, Joan Hassall, and eventually Thomas Bewick. He read John Beedham's engraving manual and studied the work of several

Canadian engravers, including Edwin Holgate and Rosemary Kilbourn. A visit with Gerard Brender à Brandis gave him support and encouragement. Slowly he learned to visualize the image in reverse and to think of engraving a positive white line. As he says, 'You have to learn to draw with light.'

Wesley's first engraving of Abi Yo Yo, the universal folk minstrel, shows an ability to delineate forms and control texture clearly. In 'Song', reminiscent of the work of Gwen Raverat (whom Wesley admires greatly), he engraves with short lines across the form to define volume, so that light follows the contours. His classical allusions in engravings like 'Europa' and 'Leda' also show the positive influence of Gwen Raverat.

Wesley likes to establish white and black areas at the outset and *invent* the greys as he goes along. 'Standby' suggests detail with the simplest of forms and strokes and, as in 'Private Dancer' and 'Panda', a mood is sustained through the careful choice of light and dark areas, with minimal cutting and stippling.

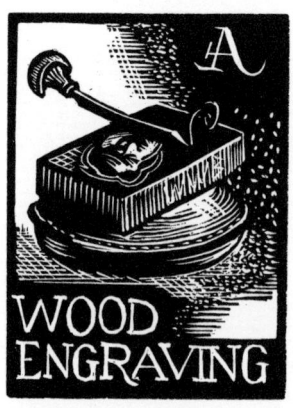

After experimenting with a number of tools, Wesley narrowed his selection to spitstickers, tint tools, and square scorpers or chisels. He shows his admiration for English wood engraving in his skilful use of these simple gravers and his ability to suggest character and expression in his subjects. This is particularly evident in a humorous series of parodic self-portraits. 'Printer' depicts the subject checking a proof while imbibing in his untidy shop. 'Printer and Muse' shows the printer oblivious to the charms of his inspiration. In 'Engraver', the artist at work, observed by an angel, is about to be prodded by a devil. (How well we know the cause of a slipped stroke!)

Music plays an important part in Wesley's life and many engravings have been inspired by banjo players, jazz and folk musicians, and musical angels. 'Minstrel' and 'Circle Angel' are outstanding in their handling of form and light, and the latter is one of Wesley's most decorative and joyful engravings to date. Wesley says he hoped to produce the emotion of music and sound in these engravings and to use engraving as a visual form of poetry.

As Wesley's reputation grew he produced several bookplates on commission, which allowed him to

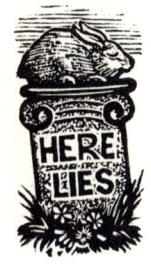

explore the wood-engraved letterform. At first he found it difficult to create lettering in reverse, to keep the letters even in weight, and to maintain clean intersections with his tools. But he has learned to work with the client to find appropriate images for the ex-libris and to trust his own impression of the client. With every commission, Wesley's skill in reflecting the subject of the bookplate in image and letterform has improved.

In 1984 Wesley founded the West Meadow Press to give himself the experience of choosing and printing texts to complement his engravings. In his first book, a collection of poems by Jayne Berland, Wesley's engravings made a wry comment on the text, with images of a poet floating above a city, a consumer tempted by merchandise, and a splendid still life with wide-brimmed hat. Wesley's careful reading of a text for appropriate visual clues manifested itself in this early book. The engravings are printed in a deep terracotta to enliven the page. Typically, Wesley created a striking pressmark in the form of a banjoist under a tree.

George Goodwin's *A Contemporary Fable*, a cautionary tale for joggers and dieters, shows Wesley's subtle sense of humour at its best, and his skill in defining areas of texture makes these engravings highly successful.

For Farrell M. Boyce's *Down by the Bay*, a series of poems about Hamilton, Wesley cut several fine blocks. 'Down by the Bay' and 'Skater' are evocative engravings that capture movement, weather, and the special sense of occasion in everyday activities.

William Cowper's *Epitaph on a Hare* contains rabbit footprint endpapers, cut in wood, with engravings printed in deep brown ink. Wesley has taken a classic poem and given its engravings a delicacy of form and attention to detail worthy of Bewick.

The Brisk Young Butcher, the West Meadow Press's 1990 interpretation of an old Dorset ballad, allowed Wesley to indulge in ribald fun, capturing the spirit of the period beautifully and sustaining the story. These

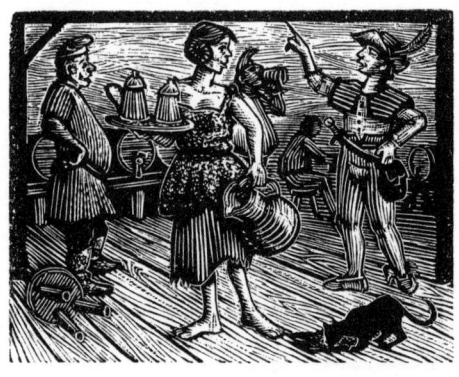

engravings have a very theatrical quality and many suggest dramatic scenes within a proscenium frame. Wesley is a natural storyteller, aware of the importance of costume details and expressions to advance the plot. The engravings are nicely set off from the text by being printed in a deep umber ink.

Wesley has also accepted several important commissions. *Farm*, created for a twenty-fifth wedding anniversary, evokes the spirit of a late summer afternoon; the farming couple are surrounded by peony bushes in full bloom and are engulfed in the pleasure of their farm. The carefully defined areas of light and dark, the deliberately simple textures, and the understated sky make this engraving one of his most successful to date.

For the Ontario Ministry of Education's 1991 publication, *Storylines: An anthology of told stories*, Wesley and Nancy Ruth Jackson jointly produced engraved illustrations; Wesley engraved twenty-eight blocks. Among the subjects are a man racing against a horse, farm chores, several children stealing a chicken, a game 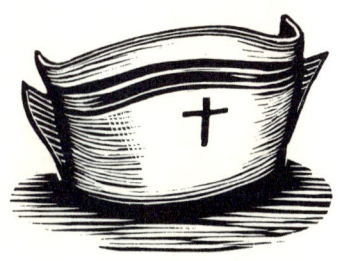 of wheelchair basketball, and a nurse visiting a shipyard. These more commercial activities gave Wesley the opportunity to develop his technique beyond the necessary restrictions of smaller blocks and to explore expanded subject matter. This commission shows that the medium of the traditional wood engraving – even through offset reproduction – still has an important function in contemporary books.

Perhaps the West Meadow Press's finest production to date is James Reaney's *To the Avon River above Stratford, Canada*, with three colours printed throughout the book. Wesley's engravings, printed in dark moss green, capture their subject perfectly. Much of the detail is reminiscent of Joan Hassall's delicate handling of natural forms, but Wesley has evolved his own unique style to evoke rural southern Ontario. His *tour de force* is the engraving of the centre spread, combining three separate blocks to produce a marvellous bird's-eye view of farm and river. (Throughout the text, the linoleum-block river flows serenely and unobtrusively behind the text: a tricky design element totally controlled.) These engravings show Wesley's observant understanding of nature.

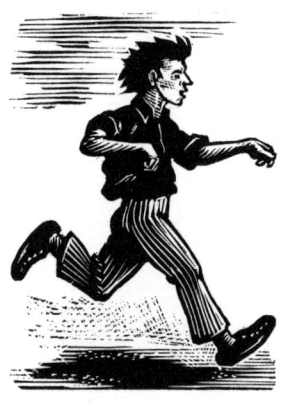

Wesley has explored the medium of scraperboard for some commercial work, but he always returns to the challenge of the graver and the endgrain block. He finds that wood engraving is a deliberate medium wherein chances cannot be taken and corrections cannot easily be made. Engraving forces one to 'live on the point of the graver', thinking carefully about every stroke. There are fewer options as one goes along, and by cutting away too much one can easily pass the point of no return. There is the constant danger of over-engraving in a specific area. One must always work to maintain the balance and integrity of the engraving and be prepared to alter plans if an error occurs.

But the positive aspects of wood engraving far outweigh any difficulties. The medium is an almost perfect complement to the printed text and often seems like an extension of the letterform. The result can be crisp, forceful, or highly delicate: a subtle, unique result obtainable only through this medium. As a single print or combined with text, a wood engraving can have the immediacy and emotional power of chamber music.

John Farleigh wrote, 'There are no limits to what can be done with the graver in the hands of the artist ... The artist is limited by his personality, and nothing more.' Because of his technical skill and his remarkable handling of detail, Wesley's engravings maintain their moods and tell their tales with style, sensitivity, humour, and skill. Wesley understands the full meaning of Farrell Boyce's words:

> *Given a chance, light reaches in,*
> *And shows the way out.*

WILLIAM RUETER

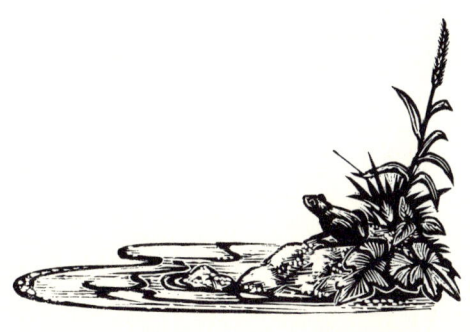

My first tools and blocks were given to me as a
Christmas present in 1980, by Katherine MacDonald,
my wife. I think she really bought them because the
tools looked so beautiful in their own blue, felt-lined
case. The steel sparkled and the smooth wooden
handles glowed. The whole ensemble was seductive the
way a chest of fine silver is. This engraving, my first
ever, was done the next day – before the tools were
even properly sharpened.

Abi Yo Yo is the name of a giant in the story-song
by Pete Seeger. The boy in the engraving is the hero of
the story.

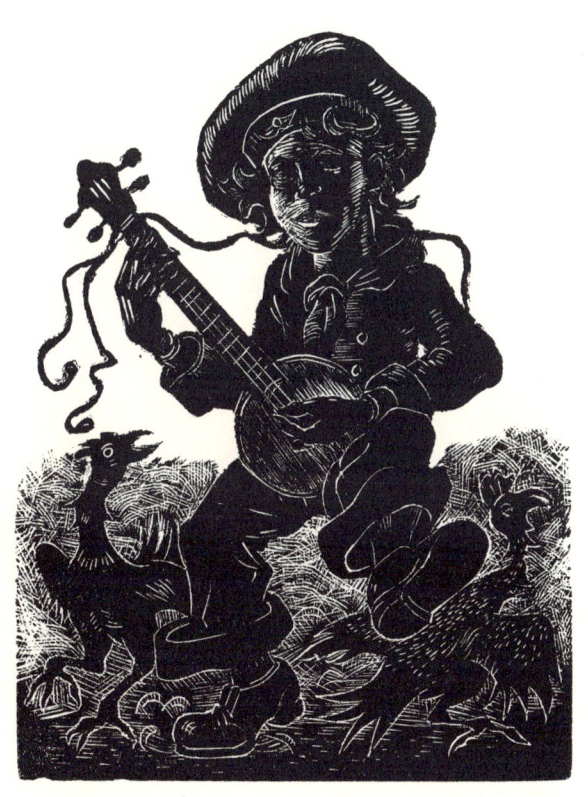

2. *Pastoral,* 1980

When I engraved this image I had just finished reading *Daphnis and Chloë,* by the second-century prose writer Longus. The story is a pastoral romance about two young lovers, and it has a lot of scope for an illustrator. I was interested in experimenting with texture and design and intended the hanging willow and oak leaves to suggest the two characters in the story.

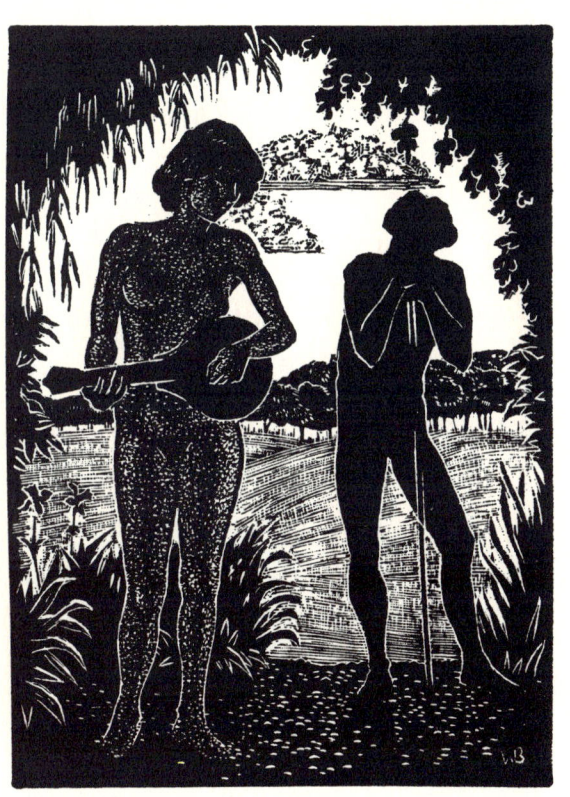

3. *Vintage,* 1980

In the north end of Hamilton there are neighbourhoods where almost every house is adorned with a well-tended grape vine, some simply trained along a fence, others creating shady bowers over back steps. There are also seasonal markets that sell grapes and wine-making equipment like the wine press shown in this print.

Vintage is not based on an actual setting, but is a composite of sketches I made in that north-end market and from studio models. I used the archway to give the viewer a sense of being inside, yet apart from the activity.

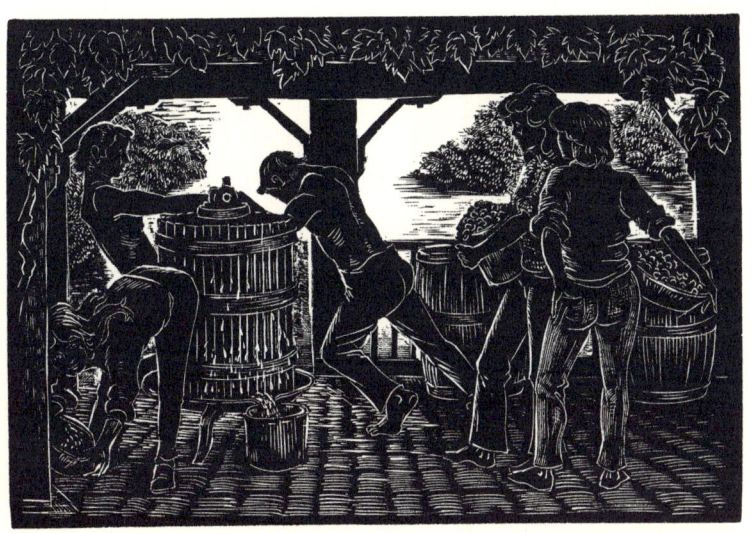

This engraving was an early attempt at something akin to poetry, in which one's emotions and ideas are expressed.

A few years after I had made this print I showed it to a poet friend, Kevin Berland, who laughed and went to find a copy of American poet Kenneth Patchen's poem '23rd Street Runs into Heaven'. My image closely matched the words of the poem and this coincidence made me feel that somehow I had succeeded.

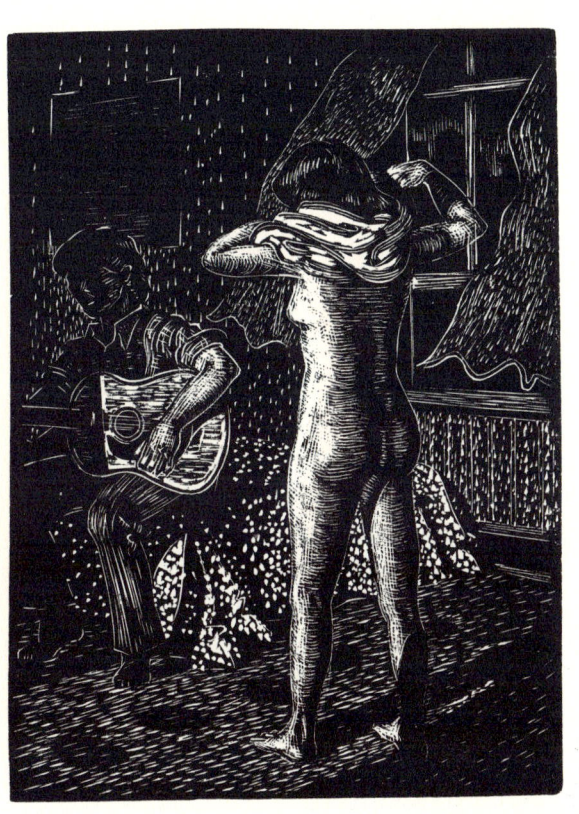

I have always been unhappy with this print because I
felt that I failed to *push* it far enough. The one thing
you get free with wood engraving is black, and here the
black is dominant. Experience has taught me that it is
very important to control the black and to use white to
strike a balance. The black should look purposeful, not
overpowering.

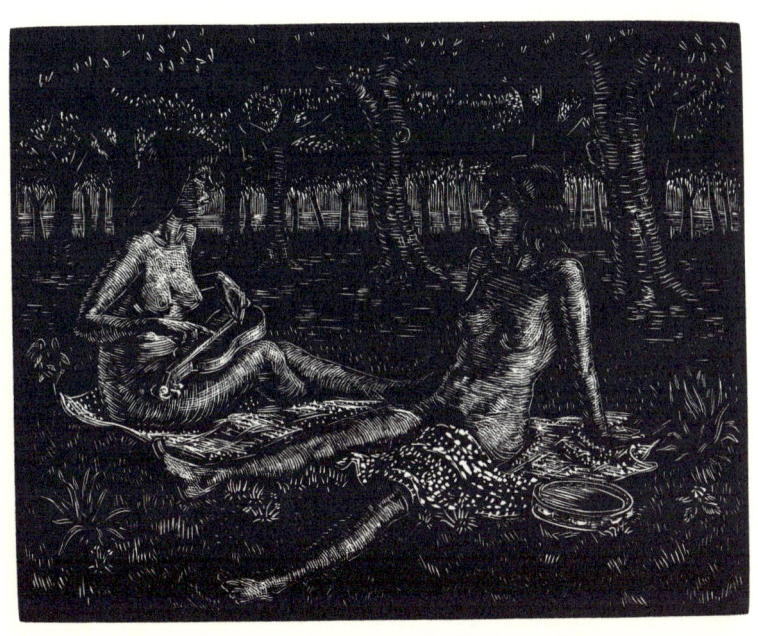

This is another version of the story-song by Pete Seeger. The characters represented here are the magician, and his son. In the song the boy plays a ukulele, but I gave the boy a mandolin, because when my daughter Rae posed for the character my mandolin was the only instrument handy.

In Seeger's song, the father and son subdue the giant Abi Yo Yo and make him disappear, thereby saving their village from destruction.

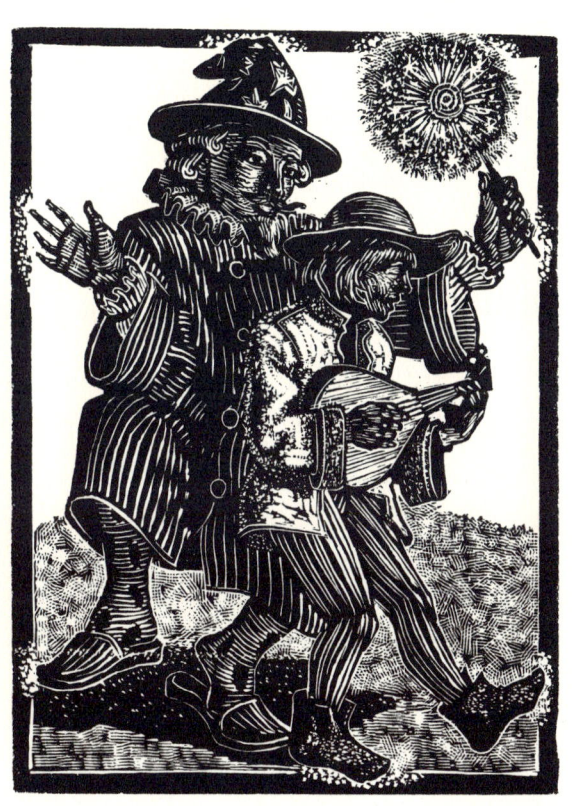

7. *Strip Club,* 1981

The work of the American artist Reginald Marsh
(1898–1954) has always interested me. His paintings
and etchings of 1920s burlesque shows in New York
City are robust, humorous, and full of life. I wanted to
try my hand at a similar subject, and did some
sketching at local Hamilton strip clubs, but despite the
many similarities between the scenes in Marsh's work
and in the clubs I visited, the one thing lacking in the
modern clubs was humour.

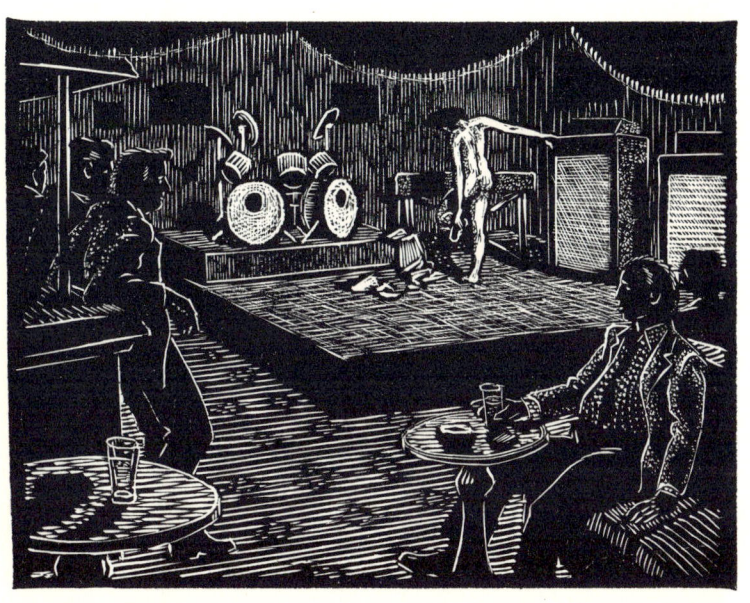

In 1981 a one-ring circus set up on a vacant lot in downtown Hamilton, providing me with what I thought would be the perfect opportunity for a *series* of engravings. I sat near the performers' entrance and sketched the drawing for this print on the spot. (Unfortunately, the circus ran into difficulties and moved on before I could complete any more drawings.)

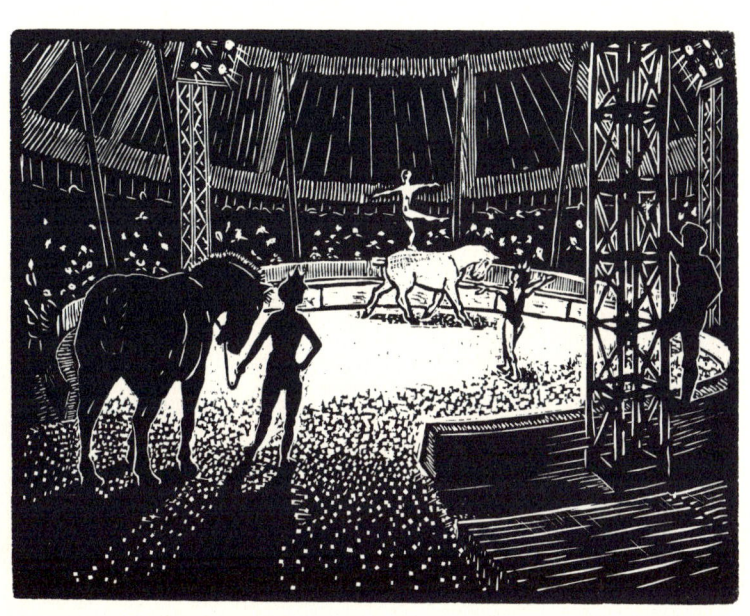

My friend George Goodwin gave me my first commission
for a wood engraving. He wanted an image that evoked
the quiet pleasure of reading. This was also my first
attempt at lettering with a graver, and it is as close as I
could get to a Goudy type style.

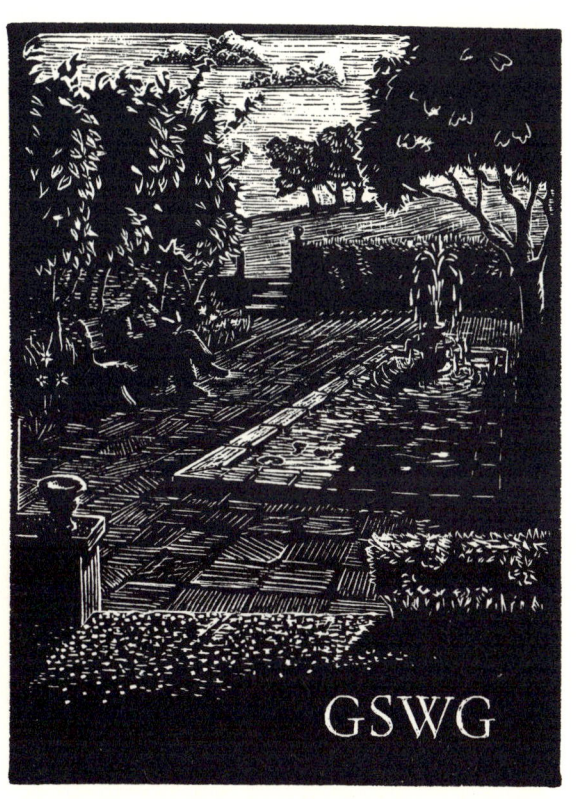

GSWG

This is a portrait of my wife, Katherine MacDonald, in her studio. I left the easel empty so that the angular pattern of light and dark would counteract the softer lines of the figure.

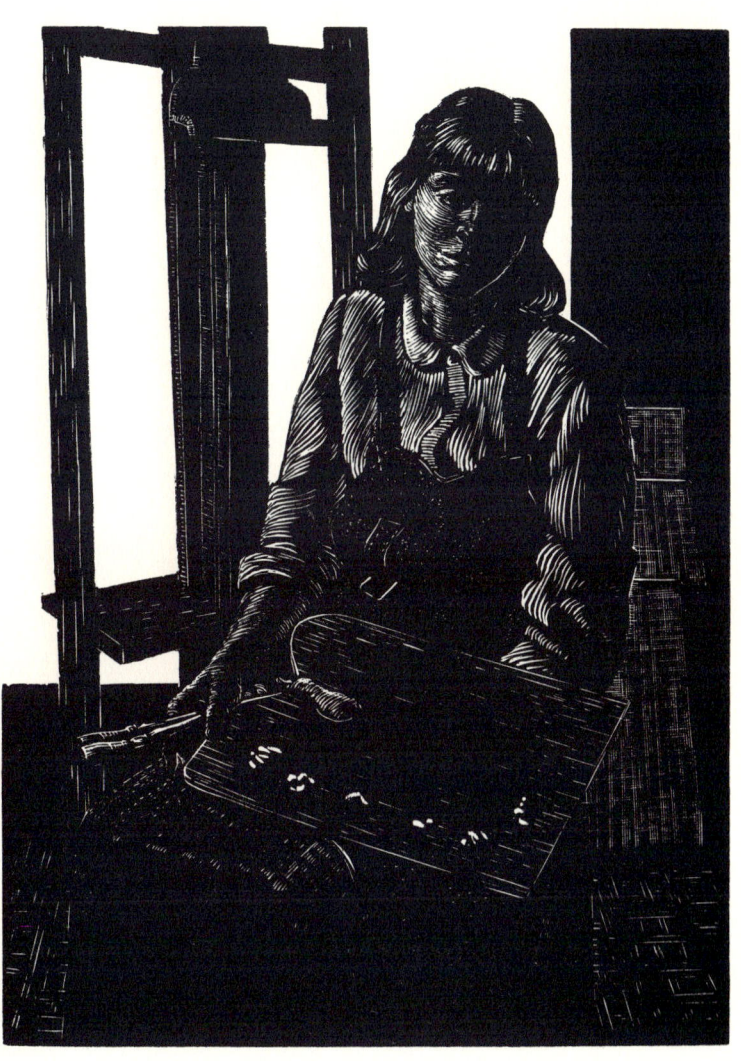

11. *Europa,* 1983

In Greek mythology Zeus assumed the form of a bull to seduce Europa, the daughter of Agenor, King of Tyre.

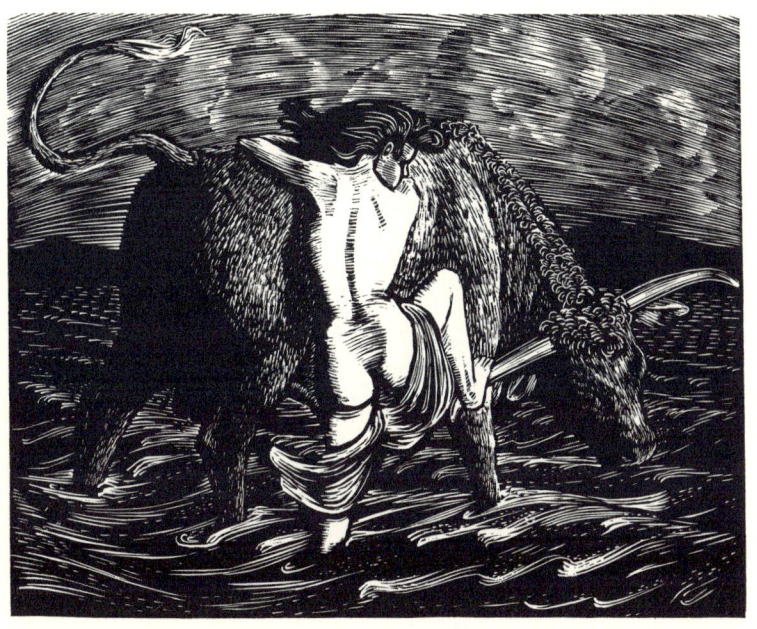

For two or three years in the early 1980s my painting focused on the themes of harvest and gardens. 'Harvest End' was an extension of that work. The print is not based on any real event; it is intended to be an expression of the feelings of release, celebration, and accomplishment that come only after hard work.

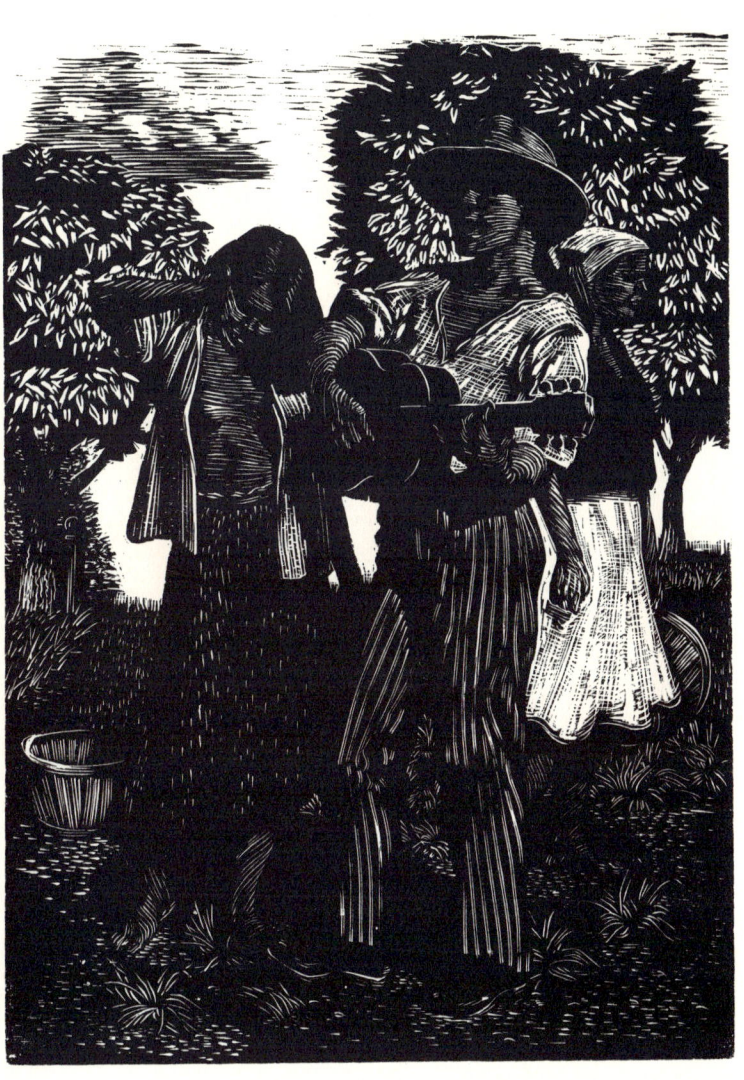

This engraving is the press mark for my own imprint, West Meadow Press. My original intention was to use the press to print illustrated broadside ballads – hence the strolling-minstrel logo. As it turned out, I published five other books before even attempting one of the old ballads.

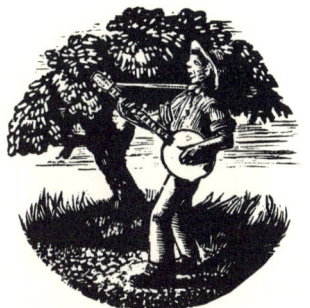

With this print, I wanted to convey the tension involved in engraving, hence the watchful audience.

In September 1993, 'Engraver' and seven other prints were sent to China with an Ontario trade commission headed by the Ontario Minister of International Trade, the Honourable Richard Allen. Also included in the package was a copy of the West Meadow Press edition of James Reaney's *To the Avon River above Stratford, Canada* (see prints 71–75). Reaney kindly provided a Chinese translation of his poem, a gesture that was much appreciated by the Chinese hosts.

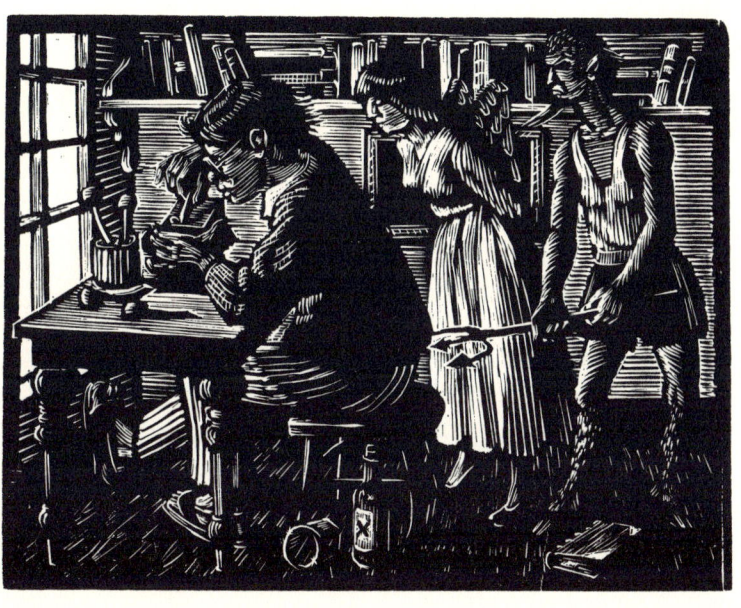

15. *Serenade,* 1983

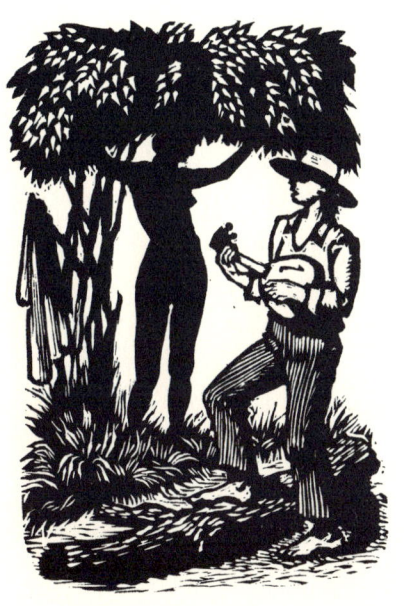

16. *Nude,* 1983

In 1983, I was working in a rented studio on King William Street in downtown Hamilton, and at that time I still thought of wood engraving as a counterpoint to my painting and drawing. For this engraving I took a figure drawing I had done earlier and reworked it to bring out the strong silhouette and create a design that would carry. The cross-hatching was an experiment to test my control of the engraving tool and of the form.

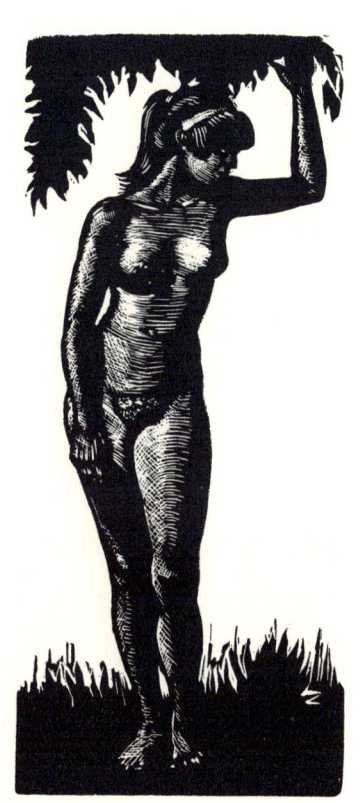

These two buskers often performed at the West Hamilton bus stop near my studio, playing to small and frequently indifferent audiences. I engraved them from memory and tried to build the figures without line, using the light source to define them.

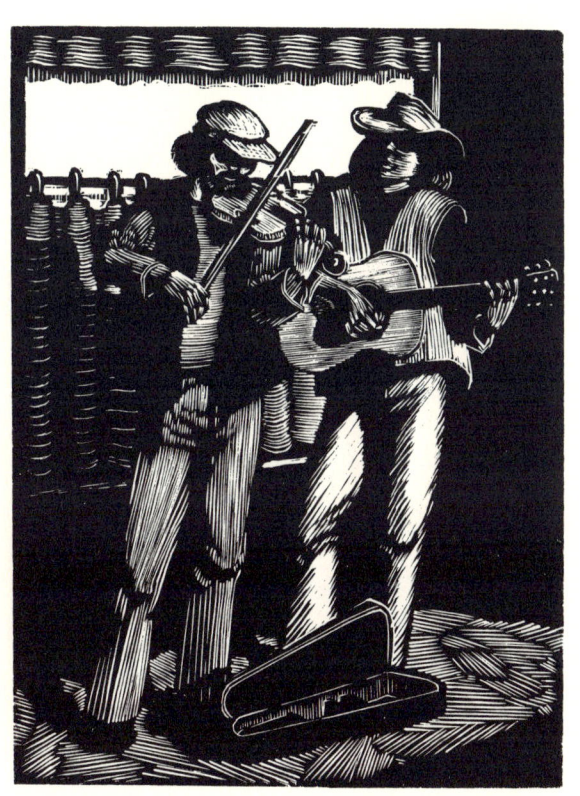

In 1977, while still studying fine art at Mount Allison University, I produced my first book, *The Taste of Hunger*. It was a small collection of Trevor Goward's poems, done in silk screen and three-colour woodcuts. Trevor is a naturalist who lives and works in the Wells Grey area of British Columbia.

This engraving is a reworking of the illustration for the poem 'While Waiting'.

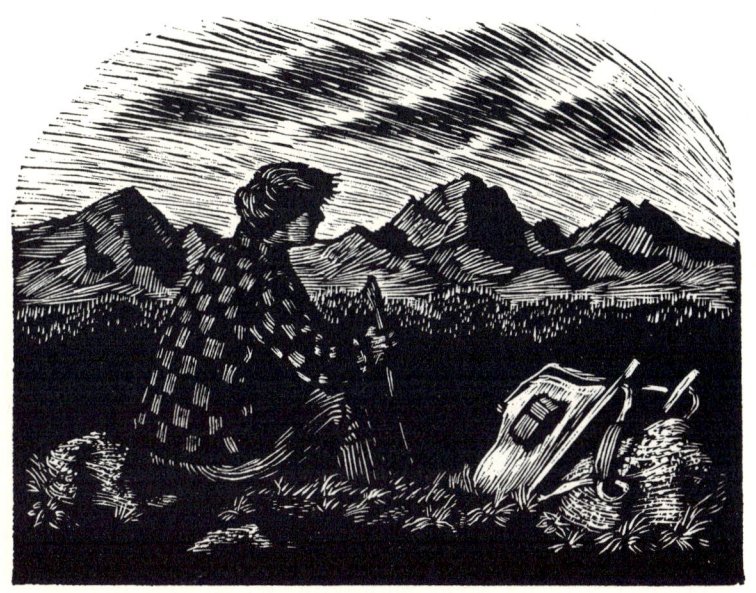

This was done for another poem by Trevor Goward, and is one of my few landscapes to date. What interested me was the effect of bare aspen branches bending before the wind, and the low sun casting the trees' long shadows on the snow.

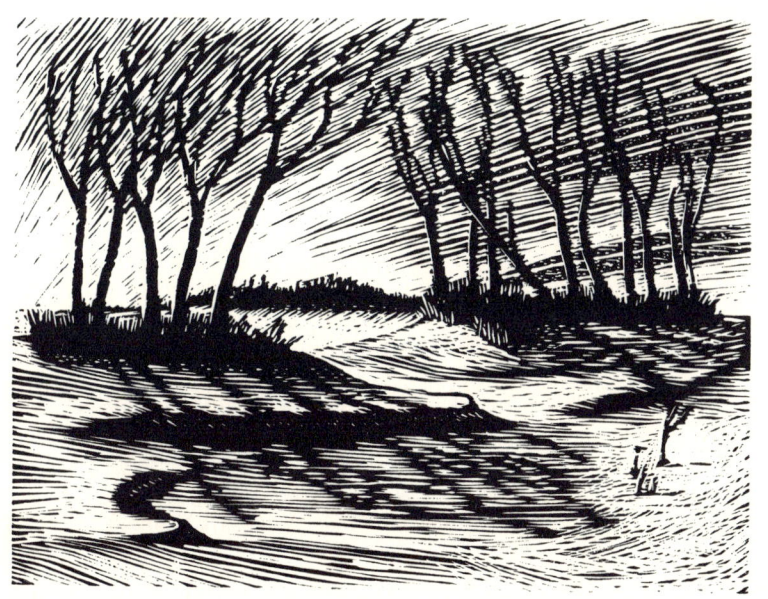

For my wife, Katherine MacDonald.

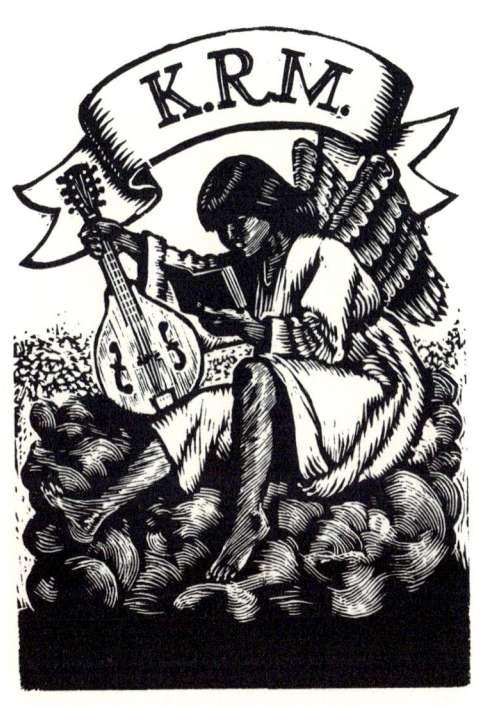

A bookplate for my daughter, Rae.

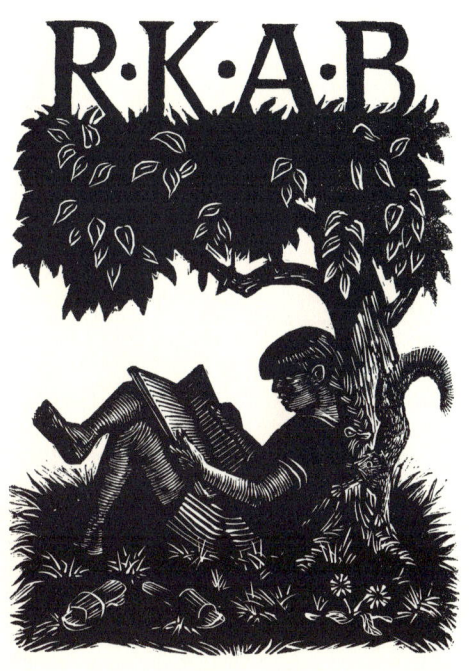

This print and the next two were engraved to illustrate a book of four poems by Hamilton poet Jayne Berland. The book, titled *Poems*, was planned as an edition of three hundred, but that turned out to be a little too ambitious for my first outing as a letterpress printer. Two hundred copies were eventually printed, and *Poems* marked the beginning of West Meadow Press.

Jayne is still as critical of mindless consumerism as she was when she wrote 'The Purchase'.

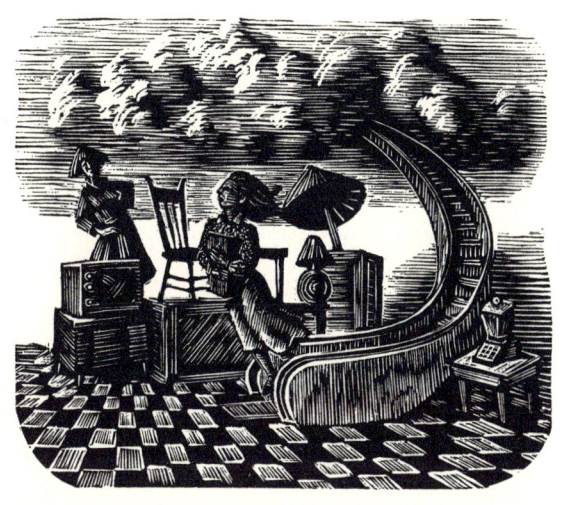

An illustration for Jayne Berland's poem 'A Kind of Elegy'. I wanted the feel of the clouds and the figure to be stylized, like those in early European woodcuts, so that the poet-god above would contrast with the modern city below.

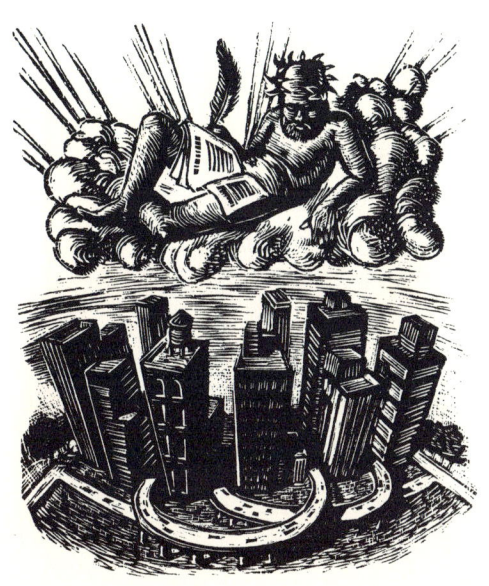

This engraving is for Jayne Berland's poem 'The Readers'. I had fun with this one, making the hats stand in for the characters in the poem. One was a flamboyant woman who talked a great line about books, and the other was a scholarly lady who actually read them. The third wine glass is for the poet, who listens to and observes their conversation.

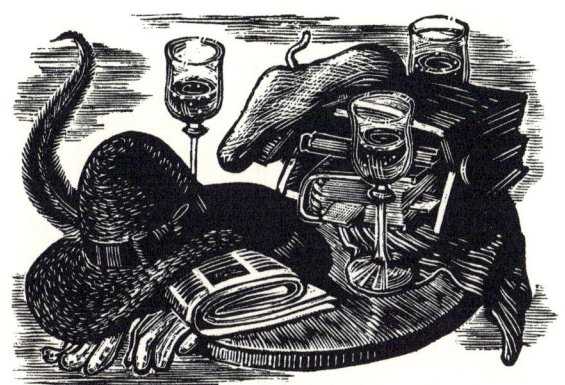

This bookplate was done on a whim. The angel is intended to be a muse encouraging the reader – a bucolic literacy campaign perhaps.

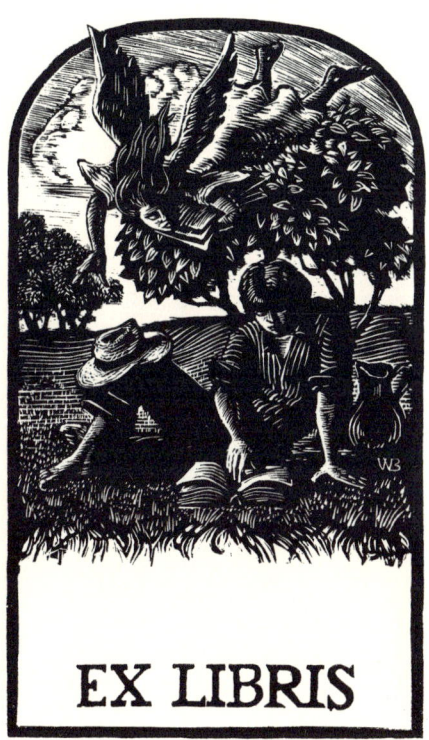

EX LIBRIS

St. Luke is the patron saint of artists. The 18th of
October is St. Luke's Day, and also my birthday.
Destiny or what?

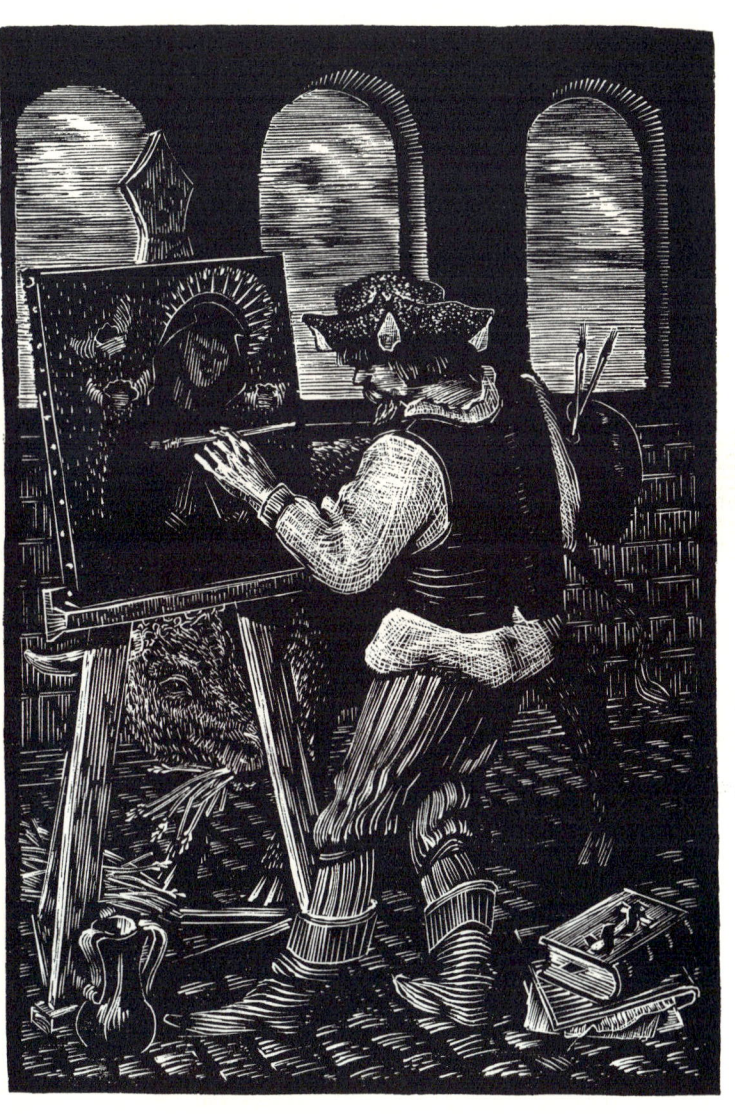

This block of a carpenter and his family was engraved for Christmas 1984. Many of my engravings include singers and musicians; it creates an impression of liveliness and movement and adds a romantic element to the image.

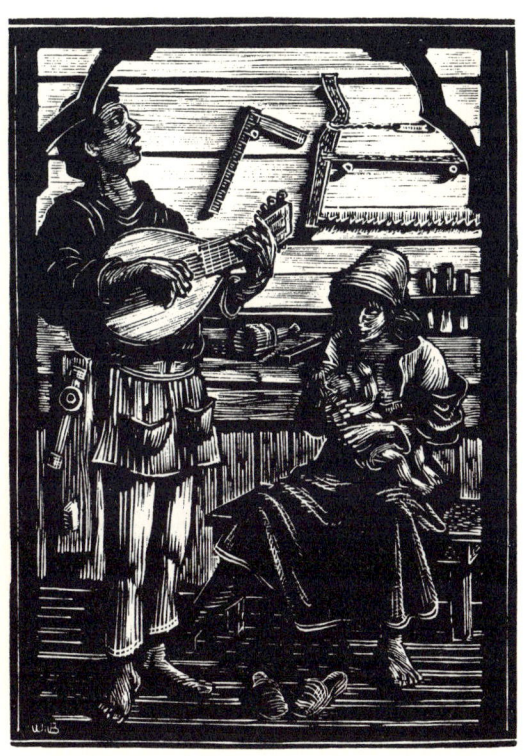

A tribute to one of my favourite books, *The Horse's Mouth*, by Joyce Cary. The composition is a slightly modified arrangement of what my engraving table looked like after lunch one day. The figure under the wine glass is an allusion to Gulley Jimson's drawing of his mistress, Sara Monday.

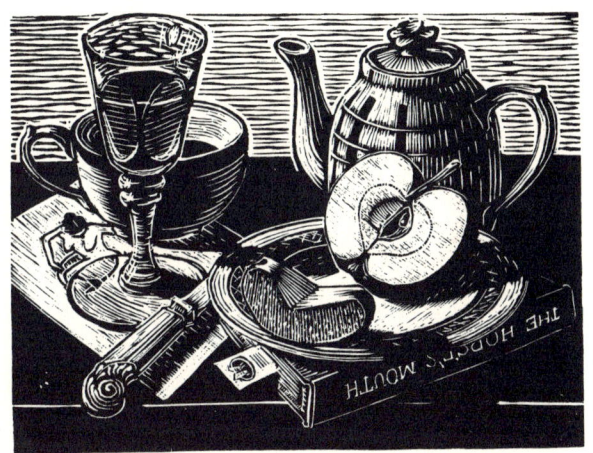

The next four engravings are from *A Contemporary Fable*, by G.S.W. Goodwin, published by West Meadow Press.
    The fable is an updating of the Faust legend. Geoffrey, a rotund jogger, wants to beat the drudgery of his exercise routine ...

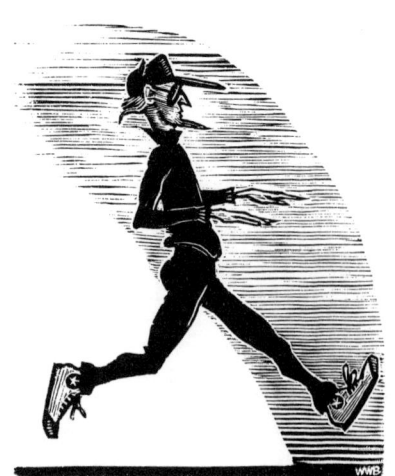

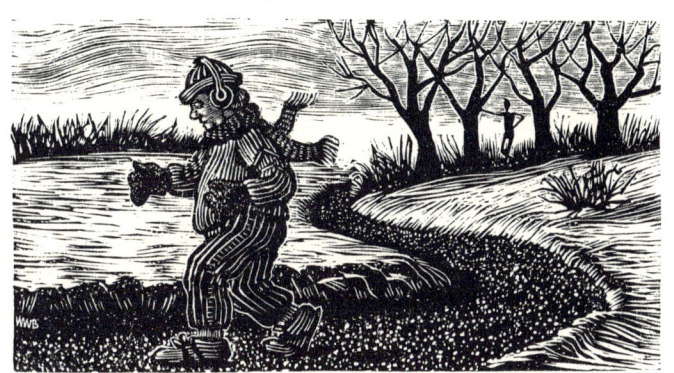

... and makes a bargain with a trim, athletic stranger ...

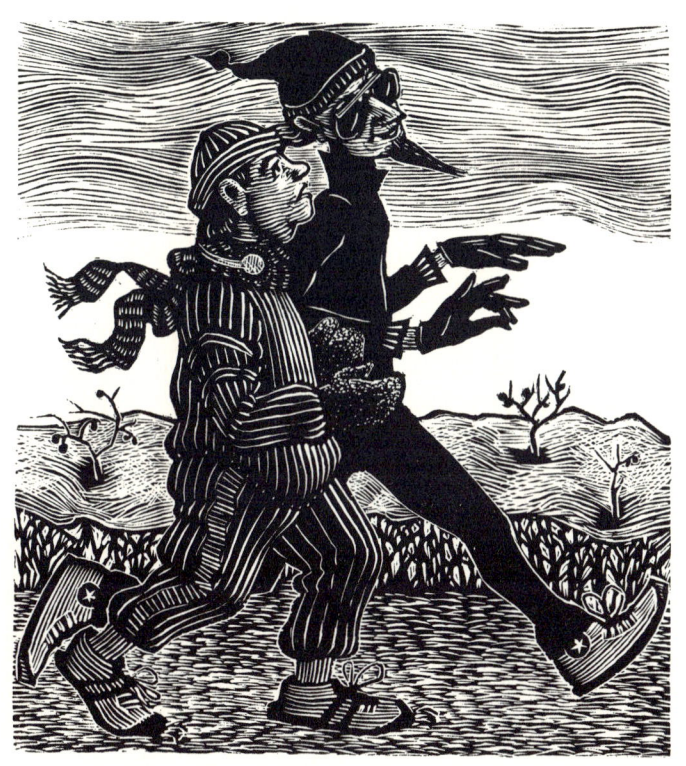

... and is transformed: a metamorphosis for which he will pay in the end.

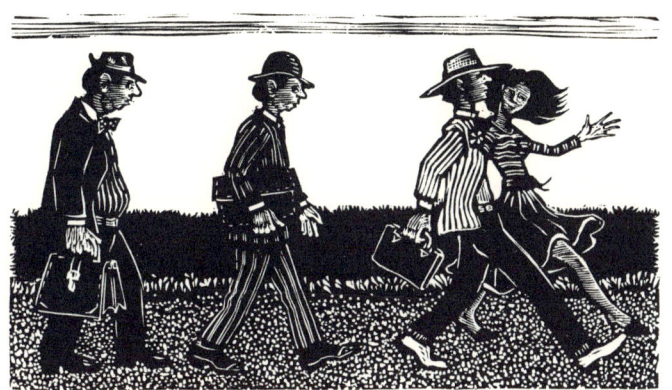

This print was intended to be the frontispiece for a West Meadow Press book to be called *The Wager.* The story comes from an old and anonymous English ballad about love, and not-so-honourable intentions. Alas, it is one of many projects that haven't yet been completed.

I find that people of both sexes are attracted to this print for the same reason.

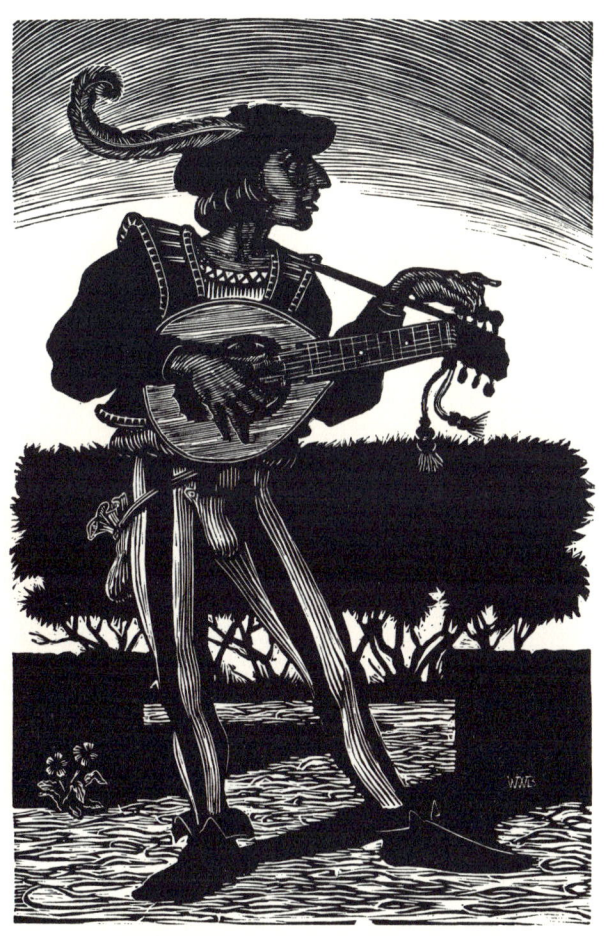

Engraved in 1985 for Wayzgoose, an annual get-together in Grimsby, Ontario, of private press printers and those interested in the book arts. I got a fair bit of ribbing for the open type drawer in the cabinet behind the printer. The press is based on a Chandler and Price 10 x 15.

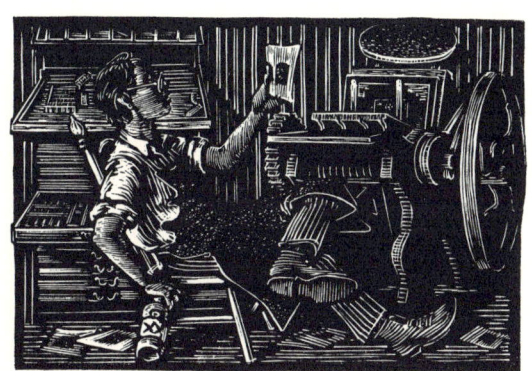

35. *The Butcher,* 1985

This was a trial run at the character of the butcher in the old ballad 'The Brisk Young Butcher'. I later reworked the character and finally printed it as a book in 1990 (see prints 57–60).

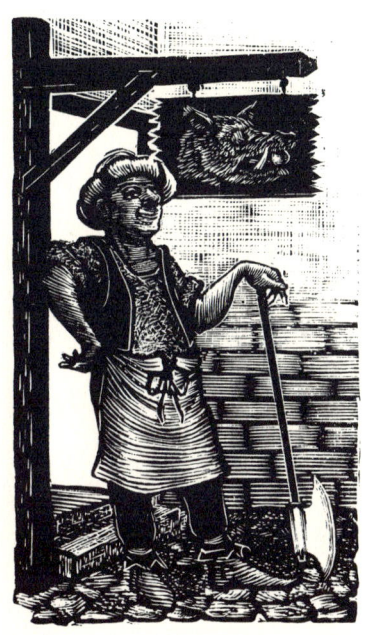

Commissioned by Libby Toews of Dundas, Ontario, for her husband, Lorne, who is a fine portrait and figure painter.

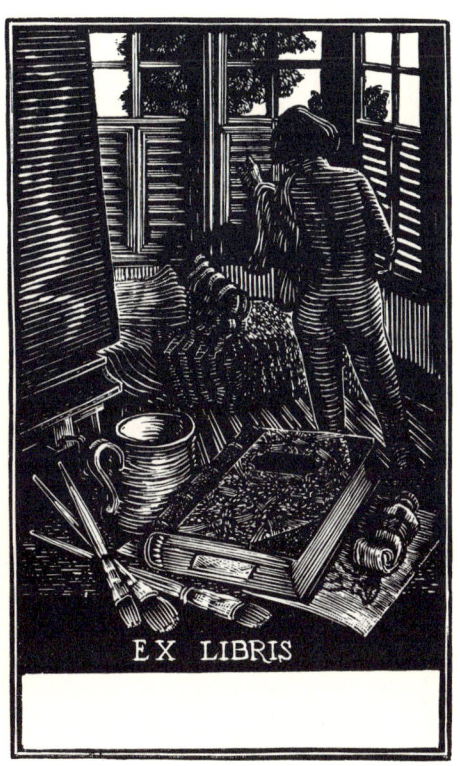

EX LIBRIS

37. *Leda,* 1985

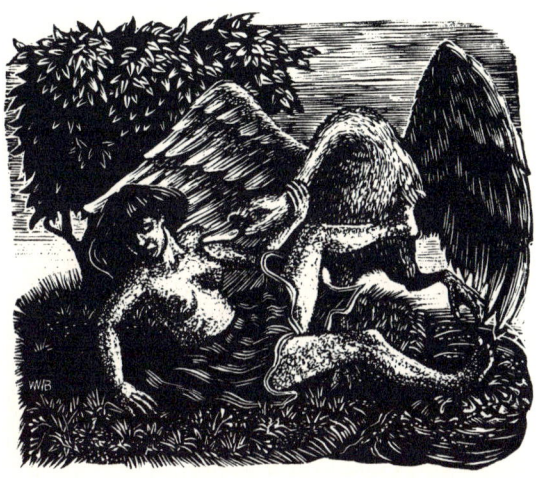

Capturing the atmosphere in a smoky, dimly lit bar was the challenge of this engraving. It is also a contemporary version of the classical 'nude in a landscape' theme.

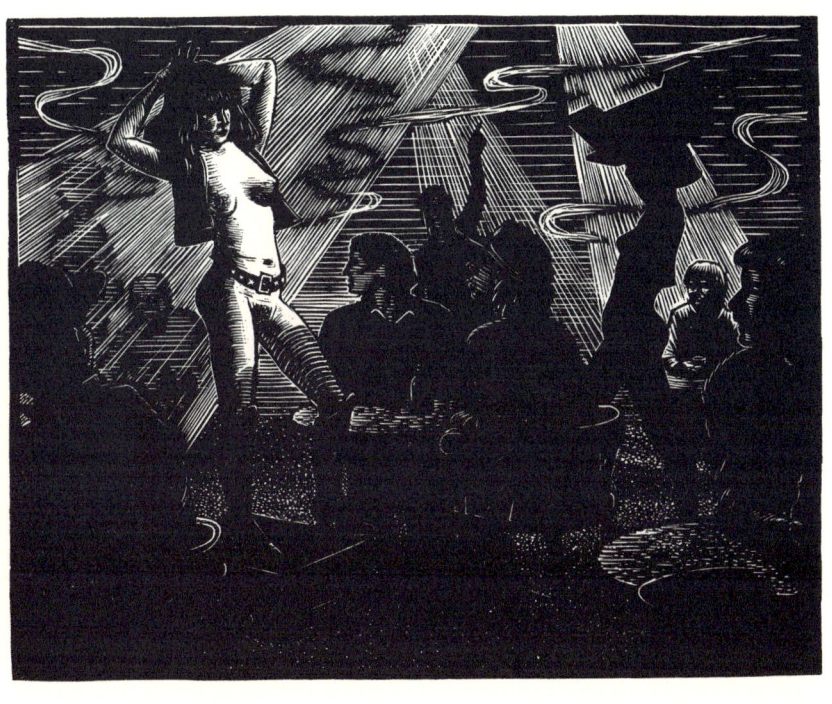

A Christmas angel.

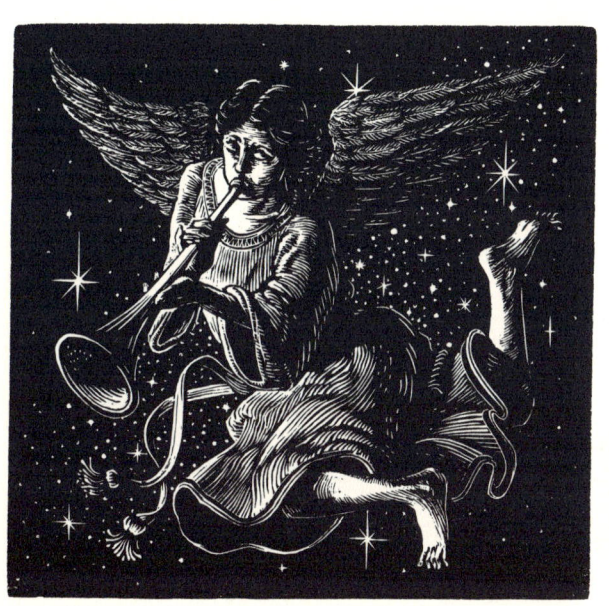

40. *Still Life,* 1986

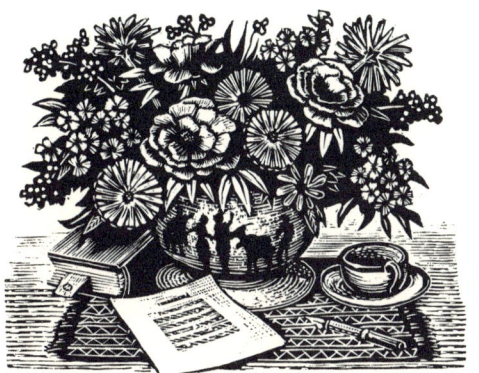

This engraving and the next four are illustrations for a small collection of poems by Farrell Boyce, *Down by the Bay*, which was published by West Meadow Press in 1986. This print owes its setting to a skating party organized by Farrell and his wife, Penny, on the marsh in Hamilton called Cootes Paradise. It accompanied the poem 'December Sunset'.

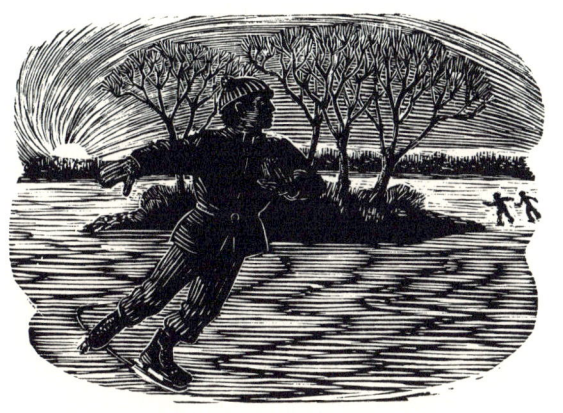

Farrell Boyce, an environmentalist who lives and works in Burlington, Ontario, used nearby Hamilton Bay as the inspiration for this series of poems. Anyone who knows the Bay will recognize this as a view of the north shore with skaters and ice-boats.

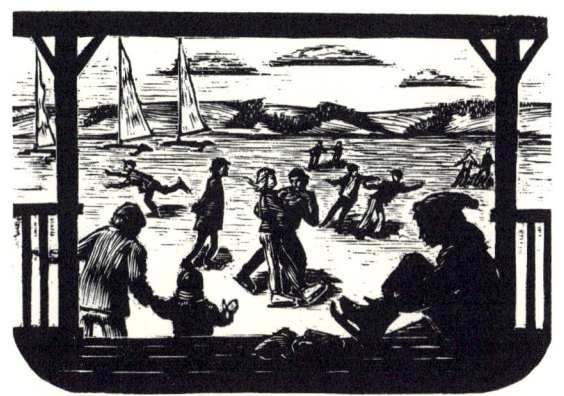

The first two engravings were done for Boyce's poem 'Summer Night on Hamilton Harbour'.

'Underwater' illustrated the poem 'The Bullhead Song'.

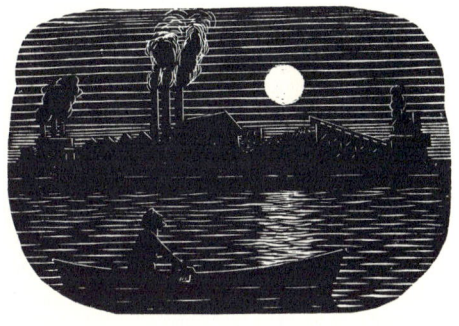

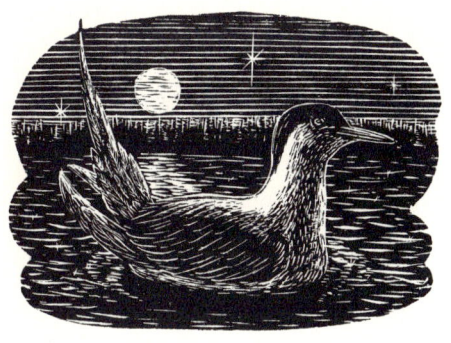

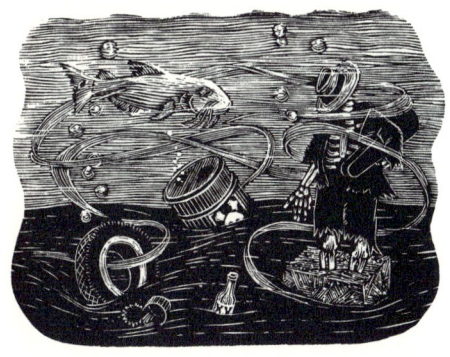

I do most of my printing on a #15 Challenge Proof Press. However, the old Chandler and Price 10 x 15 has many more curves and round bits, so I included it in this print to give it more 'sex appeal' for the printing crowd.

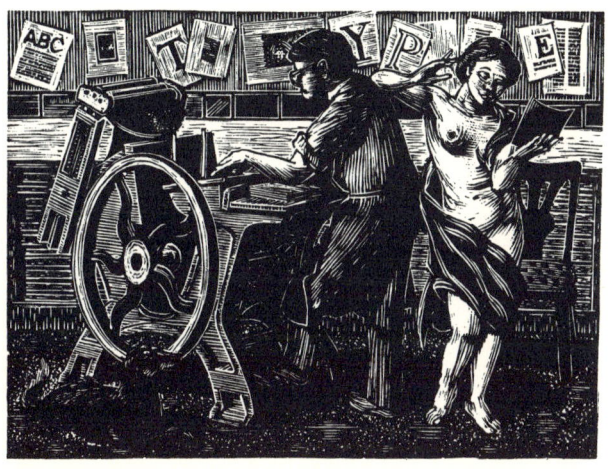

In 1986, Roger Burford Mason of Dodman Press in
Hitchin, Hertfordshire, England (now living in
Toronto), published *Solos*, an anthology of poems on
jazz. He asked me to engrave a few images to
accompany the poems and, fortunately, my mother-in-
law had a collection of 1930s and '40s jazz magazines,
which I was able to use for reference. 'Trio' and 'Sax
and Bass' (over the page) are two images from this
book.

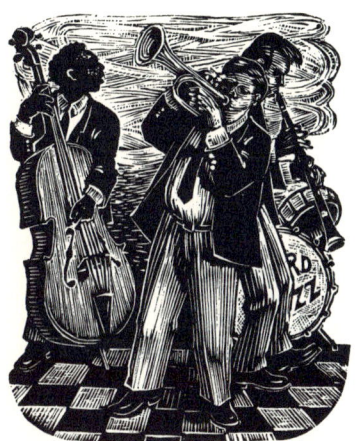

48. *Sax and Bass,* 1986

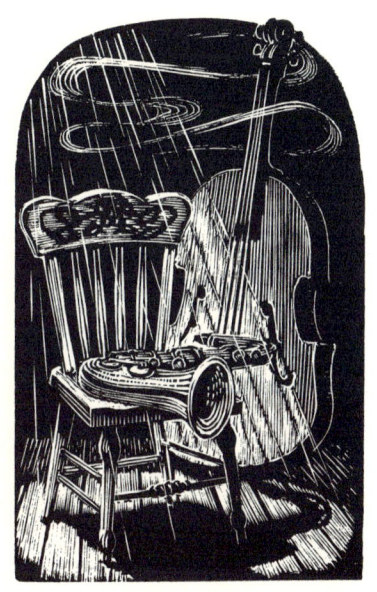

I made this engraving shortly after reading an essay by Joan Hassall, the British wood engraver, in which she mentioned rubbing chalk into the engraved lines as the work progressed. I tried the technique, and found that it gave me a much better idea of how the engraving was developing. I was able to judge the thickness of my lines, and that made it possible for me to work with finer lines than before.

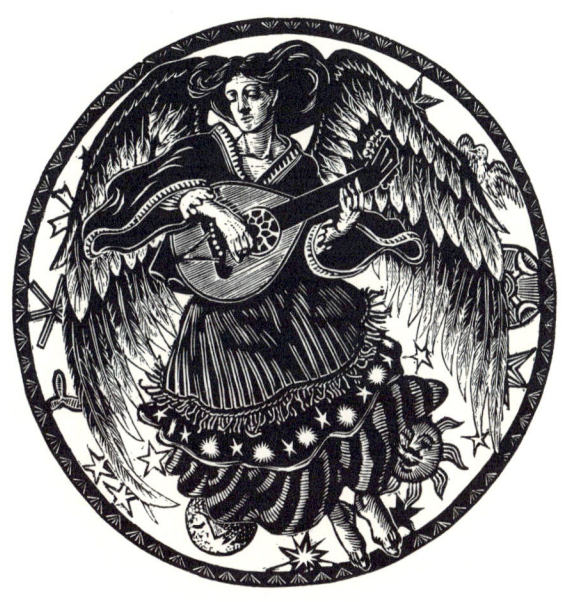

At some point I decided that I needed a hobby, and I
chose fly fishing. I'll never be another Roderick Haig-
Brown, but lately I have at least begun to catch fish.
Thomas Bewick (1753–1828), the English wood
engraver, did so many wonderful vignettes of this
subject that I'm sure he influenced my decision to take
up the rod in pursuit of the wily trout.

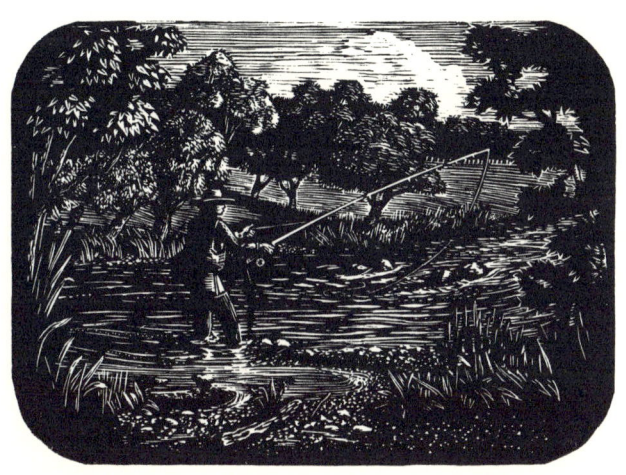

This surly old rabbit is the subject of a poem called 'Epitaph on a Hare' by William Cowper (1731–1800), published by West Meadow Press in 1987. The poem was a favourite of my mother-in-law, Rae Hendershot MacDonald, who I think was amused by the contrary nature of this supposedly gentle and retiring bunny. (Another in this series can be found in the 'Introduction' on page iii.)

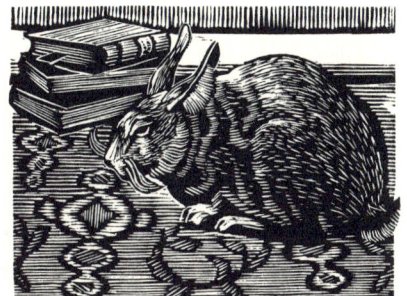

52. *Summer,* 1987

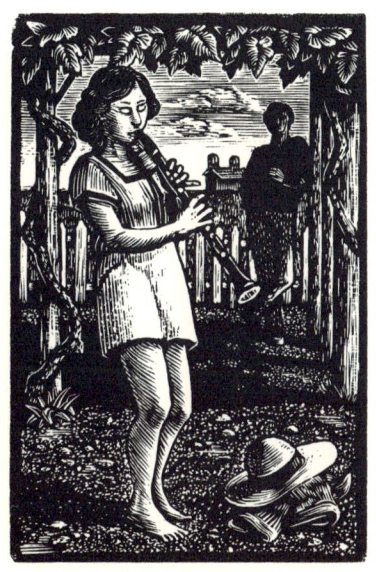

53. *Farm,* 1988

Commissioned by Grace and Rodger Inglis to
commemorate their twenty-fifth wedding anniversary.

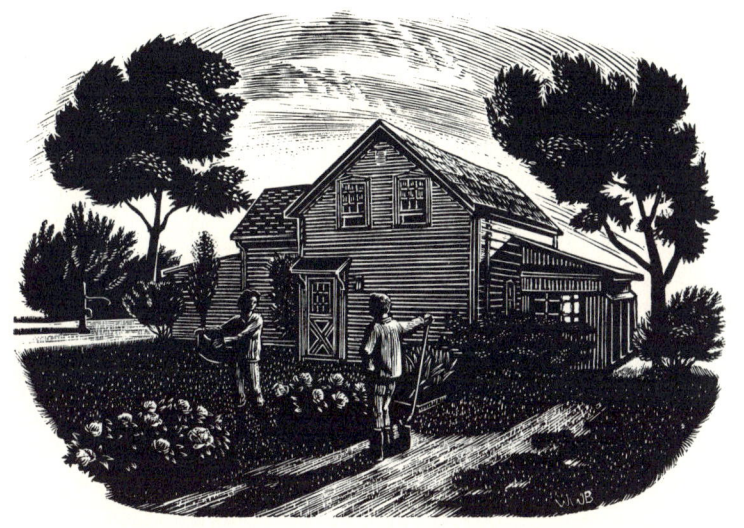

Mrs Ruth McCuaig, of Hamilton, commissioned this plate. She and her husband shared a deep and profound love of art, travel, and collecting, and she wanted an image that reflected that. She also wanted it in an edition of six hundred! Fortunately, I owned a Heidelberg 10 x 15 windmill platen at the time.

The straight line below the lettering was not planned. I had the block inverted on the saw in order to trim it down to match the furniture sizes I was using to lock up during printing. You can imagine my, well, let's call it surprise, when I turned the block over and found I had trimmed the wrong end. All engravers know that mistakes, once made, cannot be corrected, only used, so I dropped a single point leading in, blocked it up and carried on.

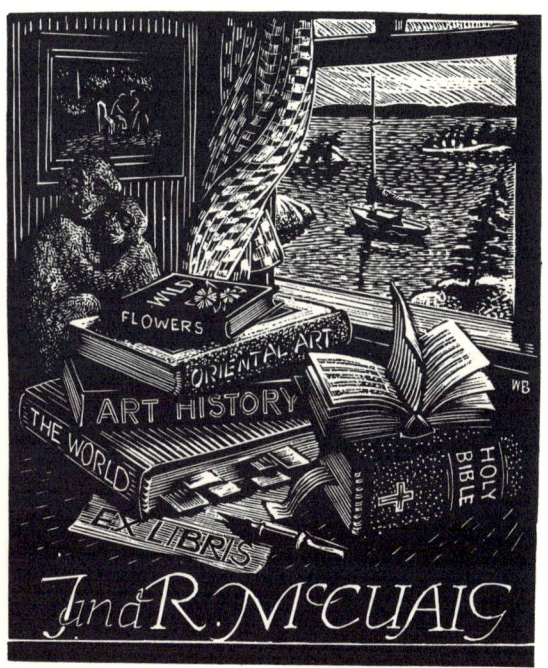

This was a commissioned wedding invitation for Agnes and Vincent Richard. The couple's only requirement at the beginning was that the image have doves in it. After a few rough sketches of their idea we came up with this. There is some intended symbolism, but I am surprised at what people find that I did not intend.

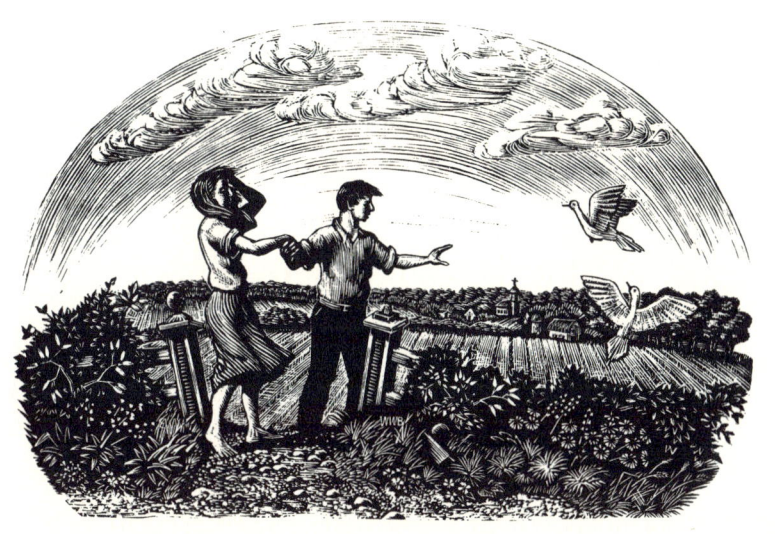

Engraved for a forthcoming anthology of North American wood engraving, to be published by Ian and Crispin Elsted's Barbarian Press in Mission, British Columbia.

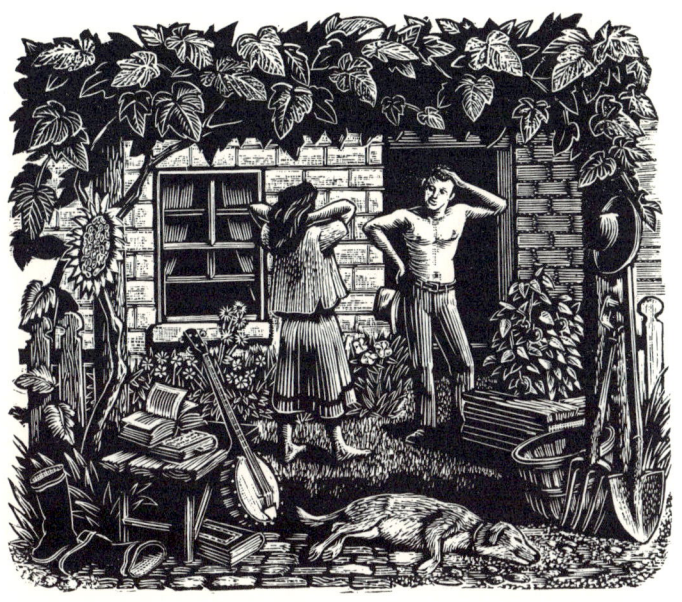

In 1990 I finally printed the first of the broadside ballads that I had intended to publish at the outset of my printing ventures, eight years earlier. What delayed me was the challenge of carrying a story-line through eight engravings.

The ballad of 'The Brisk Young Butcher' comes from Dorset, England, but the author and date are unknown. (Another print from this series can be found in the 'Introduction' on page iv.)

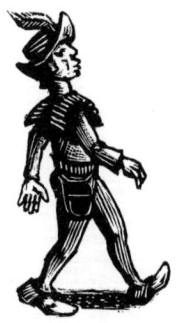

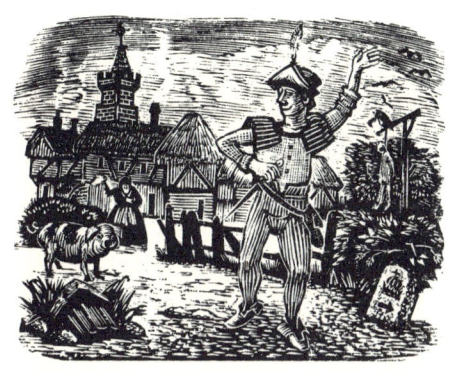

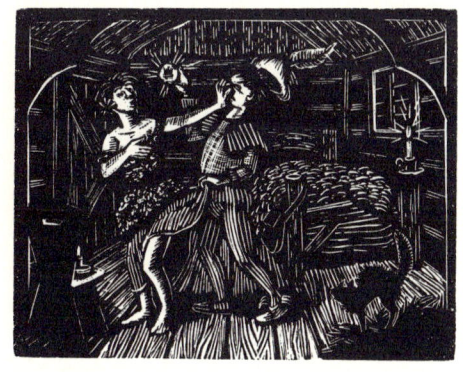

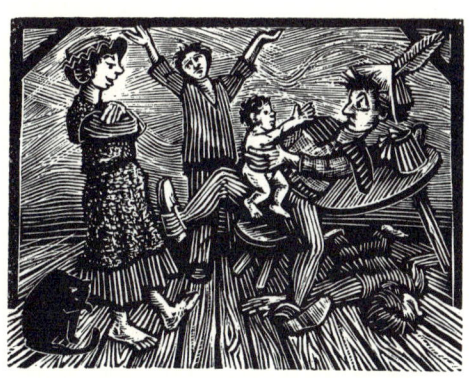

Bill Poole asked me to engrave this for the eleventh annual Wayzgoose poster. I ended up doing it in record time – three days from start to finish. Bill Poole, a printer of renown, is the guiding hand behind the yearly spring gathering of private press and book-arts people held in Grimsby, Ontario. The event has become so popular that for a few years a tent had to be added on the lawn of the Grimsby Public Art Gallery.

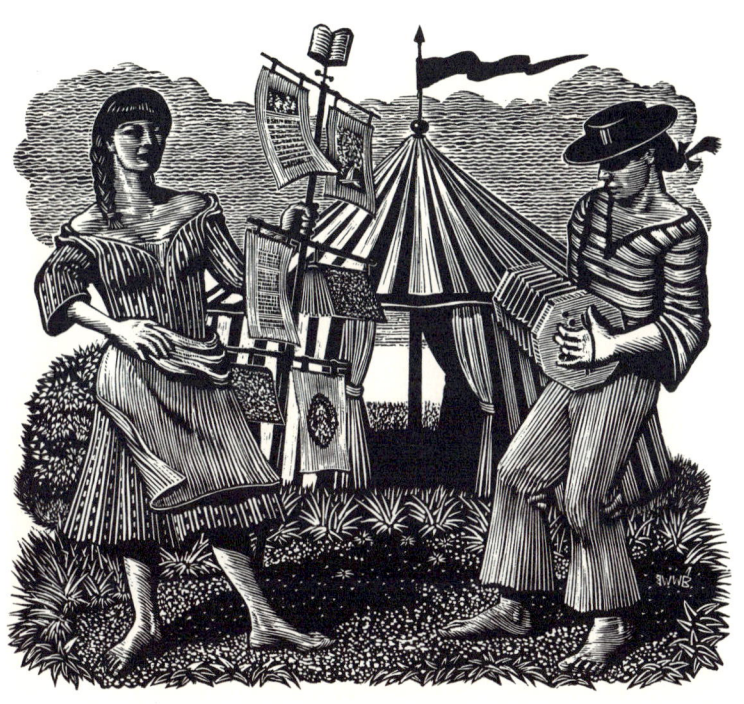

This engraving and those on the next few pages are from a large project organized by the Ontario Ministry of Education. *Storylines* is a collection of oral stories that were gathered and recorded by twenty-eight adult literacy groups across Ontario.

This piece illustrates a story called 'A Woman Was Really a Slave', told by Rachel Michaelis to Everett Walters of the Palmer Rapids Oral History Project.

I spent my childhood in rural areas and have fond memories of the draught horses and old-fashioned farm machinery depicted in this print.

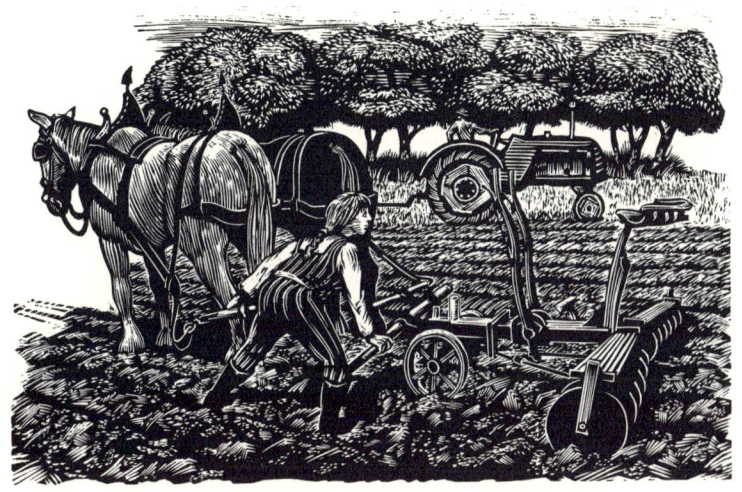

From the story 'What Started the Fuss', told by
Lawrence Sherbert to the Manomin Keezis Aboriginal
Peoples Alliance of Sharbot Lake.

As an illustrator I often have to research a subject
because I have no first-hand experience of it, but not in
this case: I *have* caught and beheaded a chicken for the
cooking pot. However, I think the characters in this
true story had more compelling reasons for doing so
than I ever did.

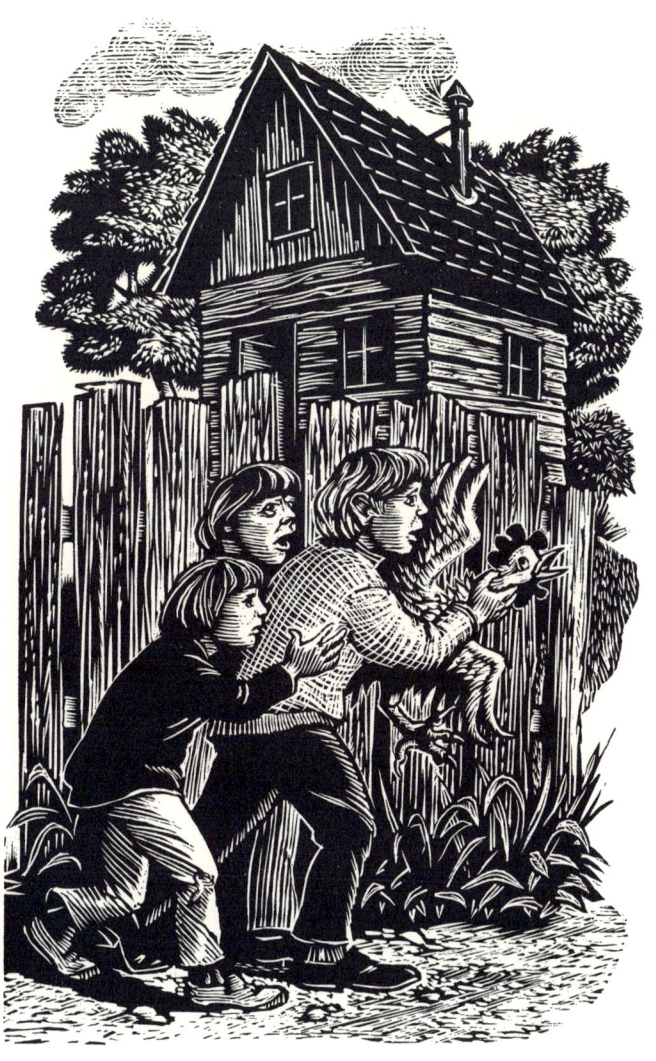

'Loon' was used for a story called 'The Head of the Clan', a mythological tale about the origins of the Ojibwe peoples. Justeen Debassige prepared the story for the West Bay First Nation Oral History Project.

'The Cat Got It' is a story that was told by Lena Marquand to Everett Walters from the Palmer Rapids Oral History Project. I think if this tale had reached the ears of Edgar Allan Poe it might have been a big seller for him. It is an account of a woman's efforts to stitch back together an injured farm worker's hand. The cat, of course, ate something it was not supposed to eat.

'Hands' shows the sign for 'love' in the language of signing used by the hearing-impaired. The story 'Who Am I' was told by Vinci Giancola to Rosalind Cooke of the Impact-ASL Programme for the Canadian Hearing Society. One of the goals of the Impact-ASL Programme is to raise awareness of the culture and history of the hearing-impaired in Ontario.

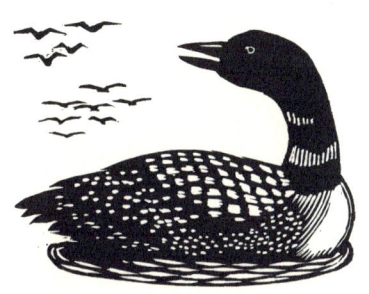

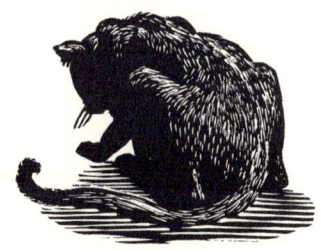

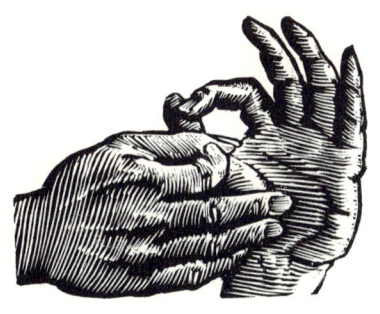

'Faster than a Horse' was told by Adele Benedict to the members of the Manomin Keezis Aboriginal Peoples Alliance.

I try to stick to my policy of engraving the tricky parts first. That way if I 'blow it' early on, I save many hours of labour. In this case, I engraved the runner's head and arms, the horse, and the driver first.

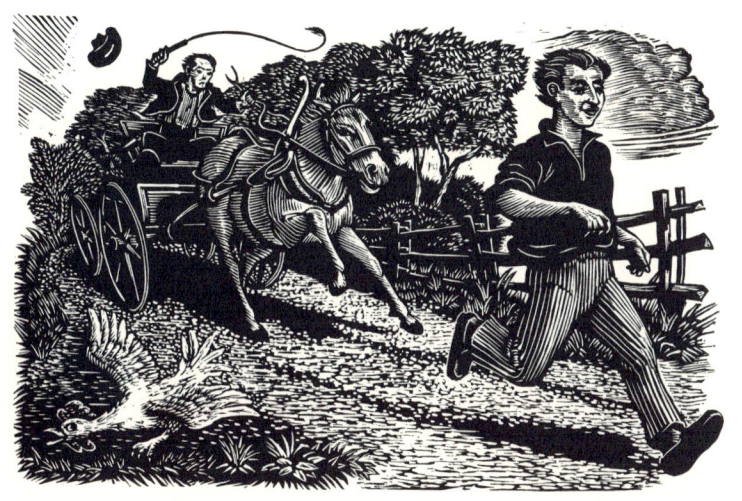

Another *Storylines* story, 'Slowly Surfacing', was told by Lisa to Penny Jensen at the Dryden Literacy Association.

This is another case where I was able to create a location based on memories from my childhood in small towns of southwestern Saskatchewan.

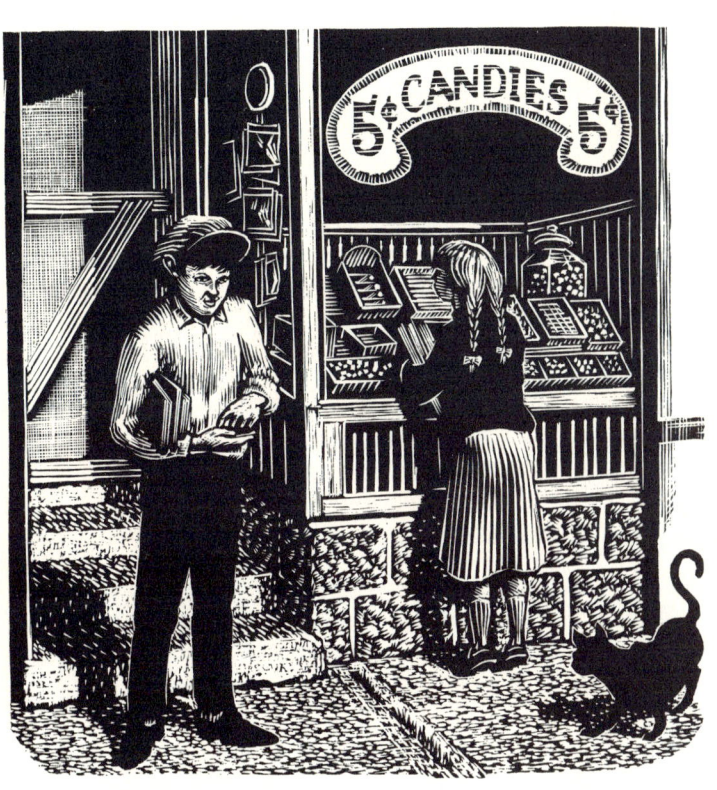

'As Unconcerned as Nothing', told by C.M. Cosgrove
to the participants of the Literacy Link of Eastern
Ontario Oral History Project.

I looked in a number of places for pictorial reference
material for this story of a nurse stationed in the
shipyards of Kingston, Ontario, during the Second
World War, but could find nothing. Finally, I turned to
the work of the English artist Stanley Spencer
(1891–1950). He did a large number of paintings,
drawings, and murals of the shipbuilding yard on the
Clyde River for the British Government during World
War II. It seemed likely that the shipyard on the Clyde
would be similar in many ways to those in Kingston.
Spencer's paintings offered plenty of details of clothing
and tools that I used to create the feel of the period in
this engraving.

I have to confess that I was delighted to be using
paintings and drawings for reference instead of
photographs. I think it is a mistake to believe that
photography is necessarily a more reliable source of
facts and reality.

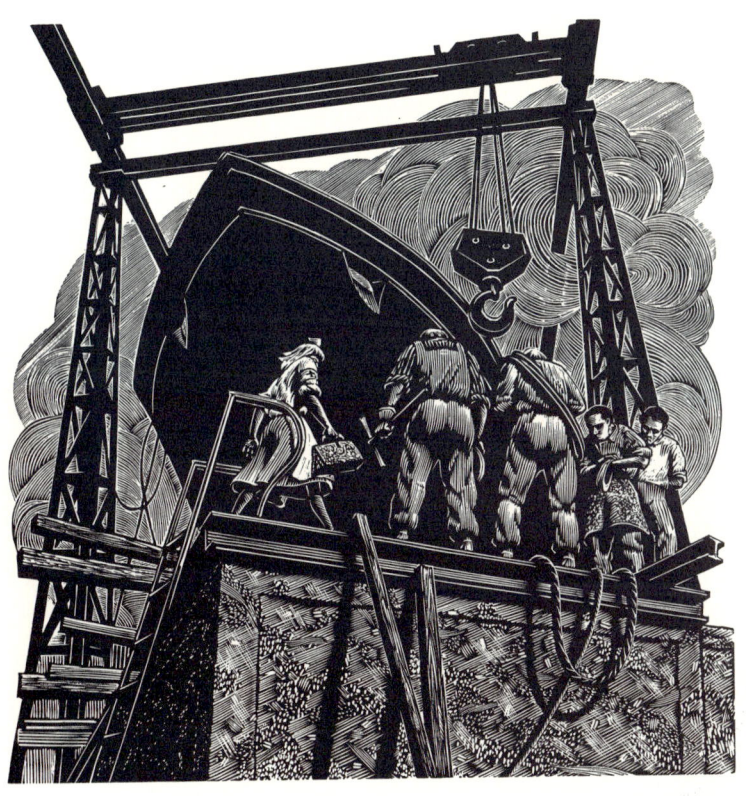

This block was engraved for Hazel Pattermore Rowsome's story about being hit by lightning. The story, called 'Thrown to the Floor and Stunned', was recorded by Edna McRae.

When I have to produce a period illustration that falls between the late 1800s and 1940, one of my favourite sources is a book on the history of the Eaton's Catalogue.

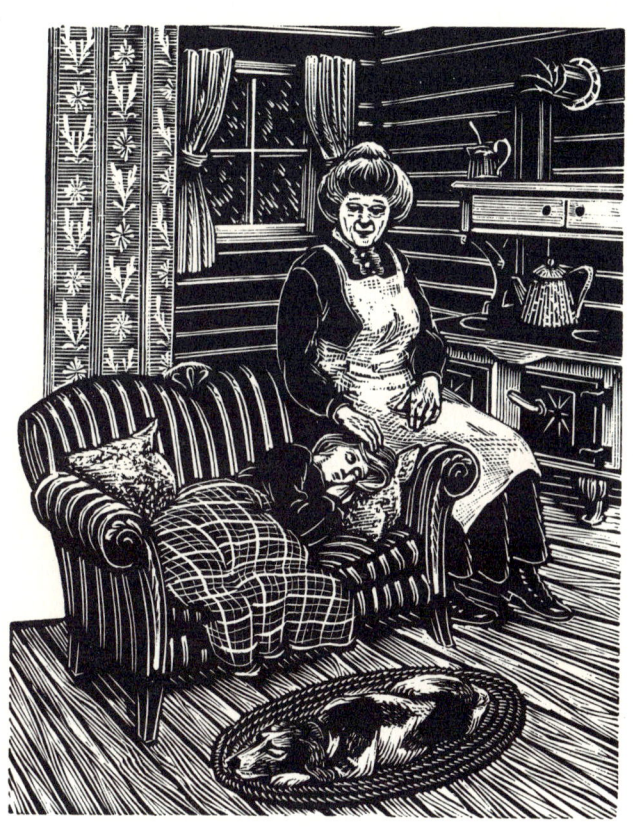

These three blocks are the centrepiece of a West
Meadow Press book we printed of James Reaney's
poem 'To the Avon River above Stratford, Canada'.
Katherine and I spent a day driving the length of the
Avon, from its source to Stratford. I made a number of
drawings, from which these engravings were done.

The river appeared to have suffered in past years
from the pressures of farming and construction, and had
deteriorated into little more than a drainage ditch.
More recently, however, it seems to be making its own
wilderness to flow through once again.

74. *Crest,* 1991

Crest device for James Reaney's *To the Avon River above Stratford, Canada.*

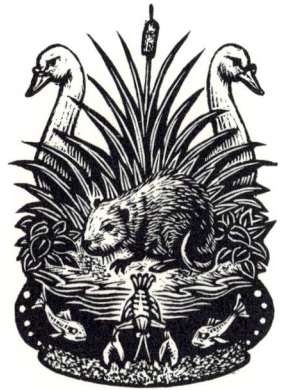

75. *Boy & Stream*, 1991

From *To the Avon River above Stratford, Canada.*

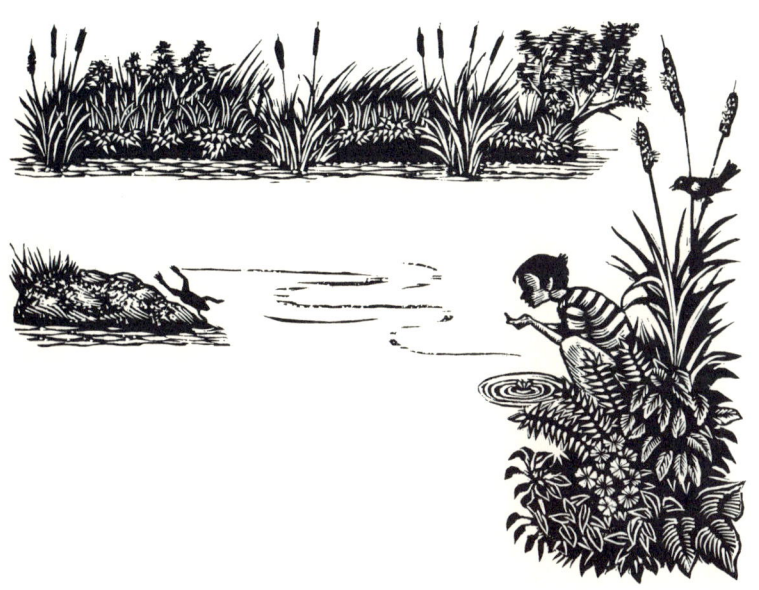

This was commissioned for a wedding invitation, and also to mark the bride and groom's move to a house in the country.

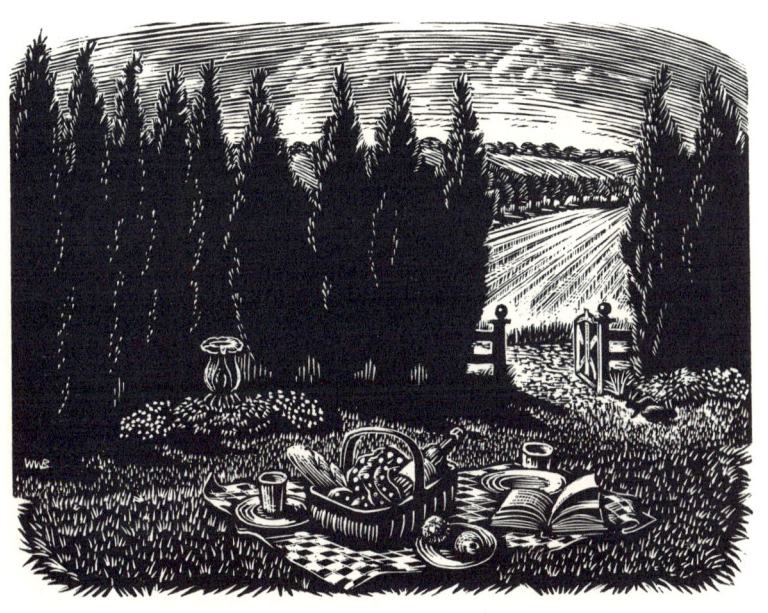

Linda Bronfman wanted a bookplate to reflect her extensive travels, but I enjoy the notion that, with the right book, travel is also possible without ever leaving home.

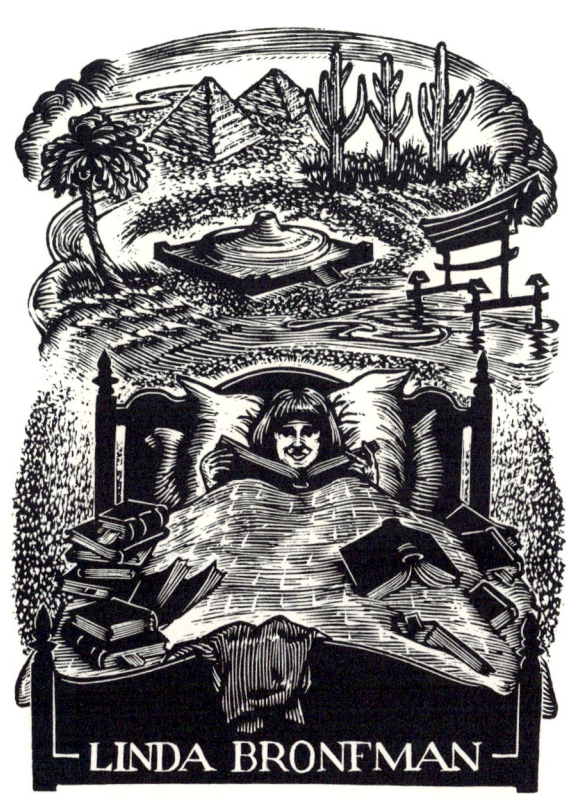

LINDA BRONFMAN

This is one of four engravings on the theme of the seasons. At the time of this book's printing, only one of the set was finished.

I used 'Fall' when I printed the cover for the Fall 1992 edition of the printing-arts journal *The Devil's Artisan*.

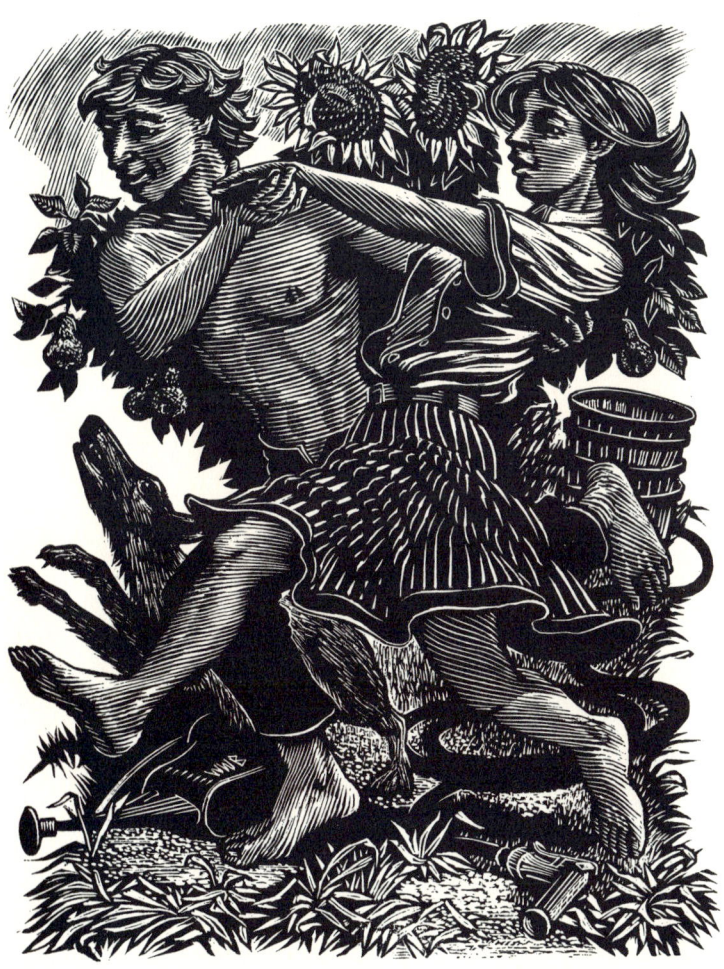

From my studio window I watch these rogues in our garden as they bully the smaller sparrows and wrens. I printed this engraving black, then hand-tinted the eye bright yellow.

'Grackle' was used on the cover of *Under the Beaks of Millions* by Cornelia Hornosty, published by Borealis Press.

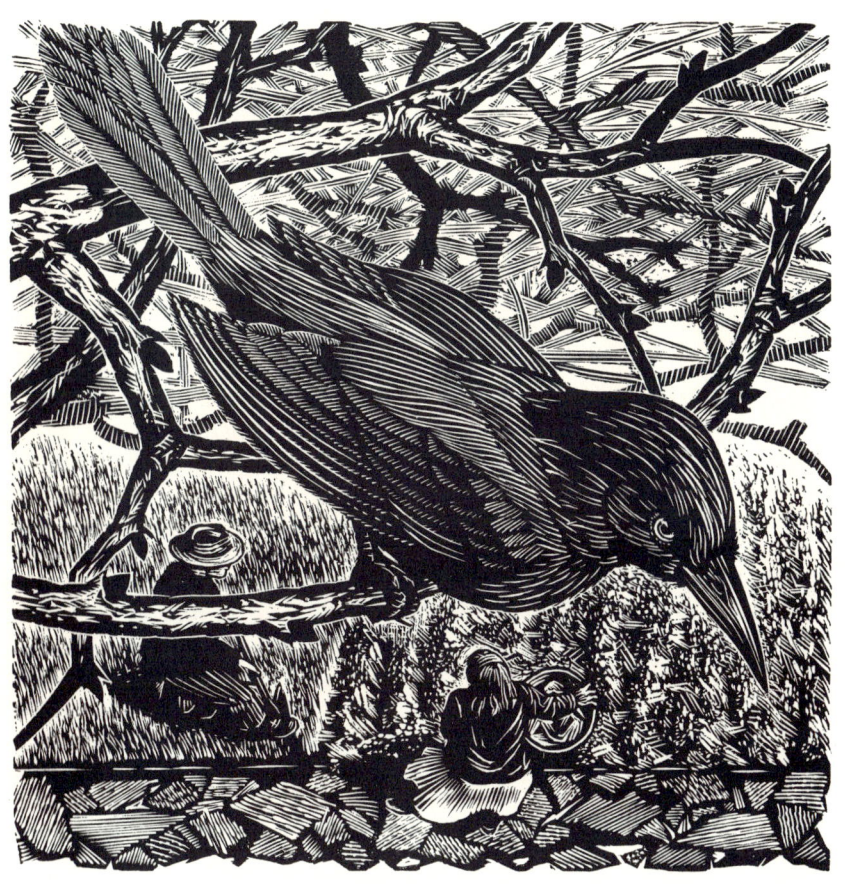

Mogul was a circus elephant that died in a shipwreck off the coast of New Brunswick in 1836. He was the subject of Richard Outram's collection of poems, *Mogul Recollected*, published by The Porcupine's Quill in 1993. This engraving was commissioned for the cover.

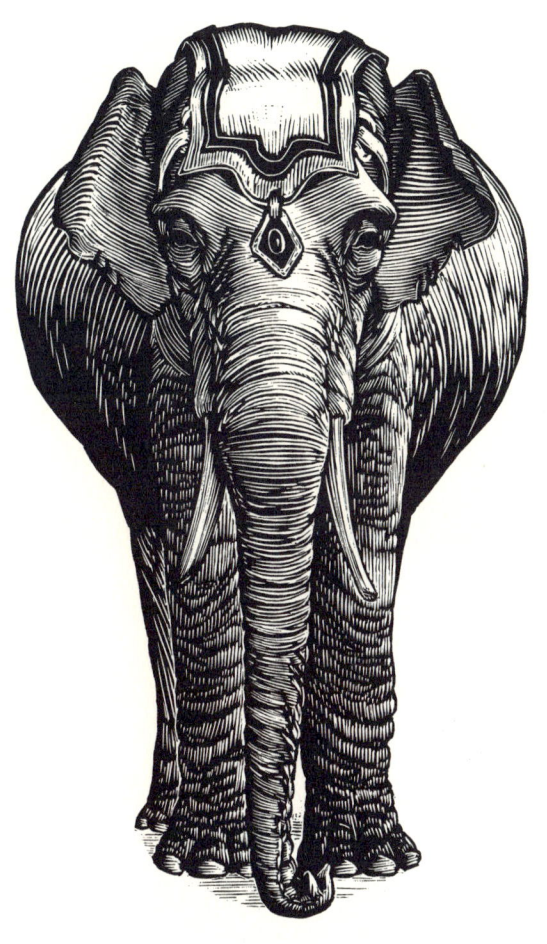

Engraving this piece was a thrill for me. In 1993 I had the good fortune to be asked to illustrate a new book by W.O. Mitchell, *The Black Bonspiel of Willie MacCrimmon*, published by McClelland & Stewart.

During the early stages, when rough drawings were going back and forth, W.O. Mitchell noticed the tail that I had added to the Devil's curling broom handle. The editor, Doug Gibson, called and told me that Mr Mitchell had enjoyed the added detail, and was going to change his text to match my drawing.

Later, at the book's launch, my family and I met W.O. Mitchell and his wife, Myrna. I expected celebrities, but found two very warm and generous people.

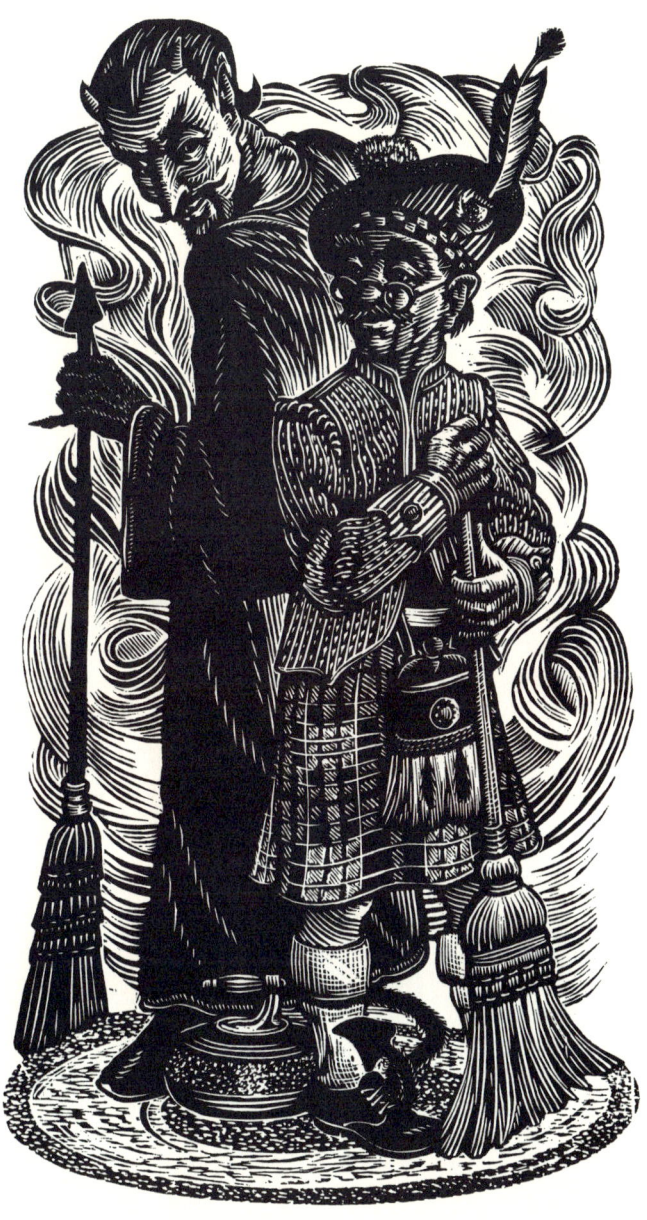

82. *Ex Libris (Fireplace)*, 1993

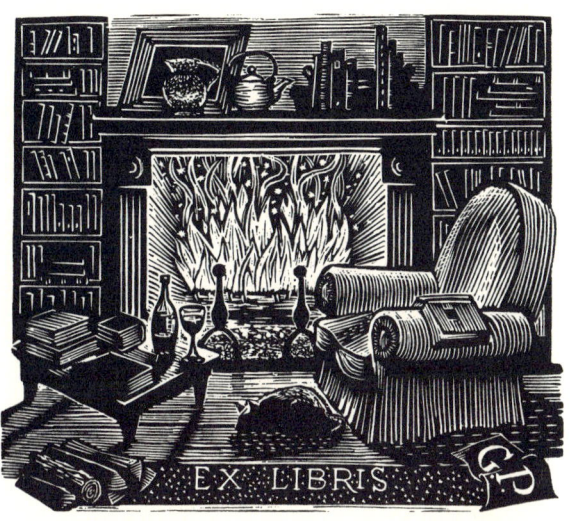
EX LIBRIS

Front cover: 'The Point of the Graver', 1994

Frontispiece: 'Partners', from *A Contemporary Fable*, 1985

Page i: 'Hamilton Poetry Centre Logo', 1985

Page ii: 'Wood Engraving Demo', 1992

Page iii: 'Here Lies', from *Epitaph on a Hare*, 1987

Page iv: 'The Sovereign', from *The Brisk Young Butcher*, 1990

Page v: 'Nurse's Hat', from *Storylines*, 1991

Page vi: 'Man Running', from *Storylines*, 1991

Page vii: 'Frog on Stone', from *To the Avon River above Stratford, Canada*, 1991

Dedication: 'Panda', 1985

Colophon: 'Banjo', 1986

Back cover: 'Row Boat', from *To the Avon River above Stratford, Canada*, 1991

Wesley W. Bates was born in Whitehorse, Yukon, in 1952. As a youth he spent time in Swift Current, Gull Lake, and Regina, Saskatchewan, then Kamloops, B.C. From 1972 to 1977 he attended the BFA programme at Mount Allison University in Sackville, N.B.

Wes began engraving wood blocks in 1980. Since that time his work has been exhibited at the Carnegie Gallery and the Dofasco Gallery (both in Dundas, Ontario), the Nancy Merrill Gallery and Gallery 252 (in Hamilton), the Grimsby Public Art Gallery, the Art Gallery of Hamilton, the Ballett-MacKenzie Gallery in St. Catharines and the Del Bello Gallery, Toronto.

As a book illustrator, Wesley's publication credits include *The Black Bonspiel of Willie MacCrimmon*, by W.O. Mitchell (M & S), *Songs to Birds*, by Jake Page (David R. Godine, Boston), and *Welcome Home*, by Stuart McLean (Penguin). Wesley also illustrated *To the Avon River above Stratford, Canada*, by James Reaney, published by his own West Meadow Press.

His commissions include work completed for *The Idler*, the *Globe and Mail*, the *Hamilton Spectator*, Nelson Publishing, HBJ Holt, Key Publishing, *Quill & Quire*, Prentice-Hall, Quarry, D.C. Heath, Maclean Hunter and *Books for Everybody*.

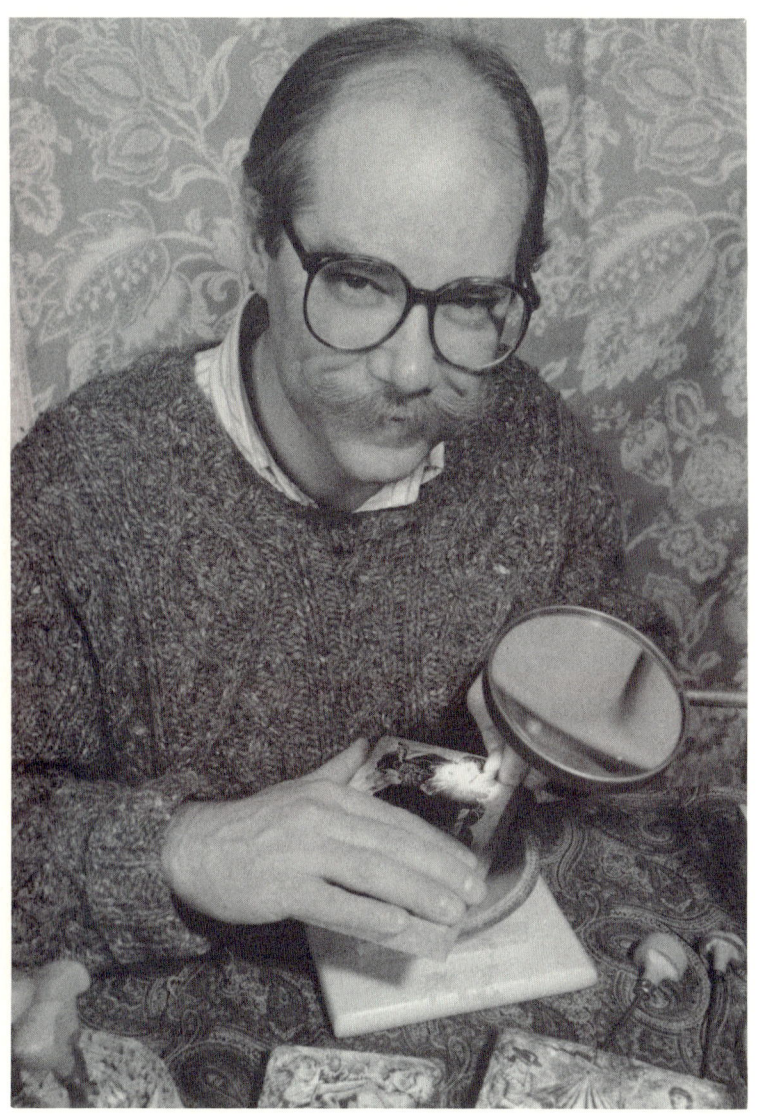

Typeset in Perpetua,
printed and bound by the Porcupine's Quill, Inc.
The stock is acid-free Zephyr Antique laid.

Signed prints of many of these engravings,
proofed letterpress by the artist,
may be obtained from
West Meadow Press, 175 Dufferin Street,
Hamilton, Ontario, Canada L8S 3N8.

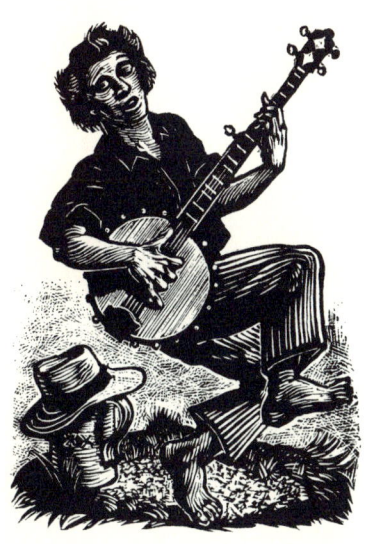